At Home in France

At Home in France

Tales of an American and Her House Abroad

A N N   B A R R Y

B A L L A N T I N E   B O O K S
New York

A Ballantine Book
Published by The Ballantine Publishing Group

http://www.ballantinebooks.com

Grateful acknowledgment is made to the following for permission to reprint previously published material:

Georges Borchardt, Inc.: "The Child" from THE LICE by W.S. Merwin. Copyright © 1963, 1964, 1965, 1966, 1967 by W.S. Merwin. Reprinted by permission of Georges Borchardt, Inc.

Graywolf Press: "Cows" from AS IF IT MATTERS by Eamon Grennan. Copyright © 1992 by Eamon Grennan. Reprinted by permission of Graywolf Press, Saint Paul, Minnesota.

Library of Congress Catalog Card Number: 96-97100

ISBN: 0-345-40787-3

Cover design by Kayley LeFaiver
Cover illustration by Paula Munck

Manufactured in the United States of America

Contents

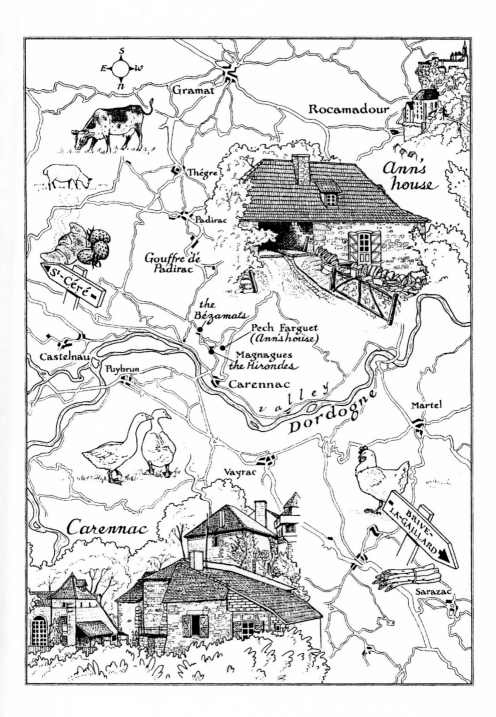

Introduction

*Everybody who writes is interested in living inside
themselves in order to tell what is inside themselves.
That is why writers have to have two countries,
the one where they belong and the one in
which they live really. The second one is romantic,
it is separate from themselves, it is not real
but it is really there.*
　　　　　　　—Gertrude Stein, "Paris France"

My deep attachment to France began in the fall of 1971,
when I rented a farmhouse in the Périgord that two
neighborhood Brooklyn friends, Joan and Richard Tup-
per, were in the process of restoring.

My one obligation in their absence was to contact the
local mason, who was to have completed a stone wall. Its
purpose, my friends had explained, was to discourage the
neighbor's cows from tramping through the property. The
wall was supposed to start at the road, run in a somewhat straight line down the hill close to the house, and
end at the field. The cows, who grazed in the field and
were herded home past the house, would then take the
route on the far side of the wall from the house.

When I arrived, I could see that the wall had been only
partially finished. I called on the mason, who promised to
renew his efforts and finish the job within the week.

Meanwhile, I made the acquaintance of neighboring farmers, who provided me with fresh-laid eggs (with Halloween-orange yolks) and milk still warm from the cow. To my dismay, they all pooh-poohed the wall: *le grand mur de Chine,* they called it, guffawing and slapping their knees.

Despite the neighbors' mockery, I was pleased to see the wall completed and to have had a small part in accomplishing this for my friends. It was shoulder-high to a cow, solid, and well constructed. On the other hand, I was a little sorry to sidetrack the animals. Cows seem so harmless and benign, working their cuds, batting their gentle eyes. I have a favorite poem, titled "Cows," by Eamon Grennan, which captures their special charm. It reads in part:

> *I love the way a torn tuft of*
> *grass and buttercups and clover sway-dangles*
> *toward a cow's mouth, the mild teeth*
> *taking it in—purple flowers, green stems, yellow*
> *   petals*
> *lingering on the hinged lips foamed with spittle.*
> *I love the slow chewing sound as transformation*
> *   starts: the pulping roughness of it, its calm*
> *   deliberate solicitude, its entranced herbivorous*
> *pacific grace, the carpet-sweeping sound of breath*
> *huffing out of pink nostrils. Their eyelashes—*
> *black, brown, beige, or white as chalk—have a*
> *   minuscule precision, and in the pathos*
> *of their diminutive necessity are the most oddly*
> *   human thing about them: involuntary,*
> *they open, close, dealing as our own do with what*
> *   inhabits, encumbering,*
> *the seething waves and quick invisible wilderness*
> *   of air.*

One evening not long after the completion of the wall, I was standing by the kitchen window, washing greens and slicing tomatoes for my dinner salad, and gazing approvingly at *le grand mur de Chine*. Suddenly the large, doleful eyes of a cow met mine. The great beast froze for a moment, the enormity of its face captured in the frame of the open window. I could feel the warm current of its breath. The cow passed, and was followed by another, and another. Eventually, the whole herd plodded before the window, some taking a sidelong, disinterested glance. They had chosen the inside track of *le grand mur* at the far end—their well-worn route—to wind their way back to the familiar barn. *Le grand mur de Chine*—I could hear the gleeful echoes.

As the days passed at the farmhouse, the lazy pace of country life took over. The fall foliage was all buttercup yellow (where were the russets and scarlets of home?). The light was golden. I made applesauce from the free fall in the field. I cooked a rabbit for the first time in my life—overcoming a slight horror when I discovered its stark skinned nakedness at the feet of an old black-garbed farmer woman in the marketplace. For breakfast, I had its gamy liver on toast. I wanted to try it all—whatever was different from the plain fare of my Midwestern (suburban St. Louis) upbringing. I made picnics of sausage, cheese, great crusty sourdough bread from the village baker, local wine. I spent a weekend on a nearby farm, learning from an energetic young couple how to make *confit* and *foie gras*. I tooled around from village to village in Richard and Joan's 1954 Citroën Onze Légère, a majestic, although temperamental, black beauty with rosebud petit-point upholstery—and in a burst of panache bought a beret in the clothing stall at a market to match the flamboyant mood the car inspired in me.

Midway through my stay, I decided to try an experiment. I would ignore watches and clocks, and simply follow nature's rhythm: sleeping and rising according to the light, eating when I was hungry. In my modest Thoreau-like existence, I didn't miss the comforts of home. There was pleasure in taking a cold sponge bath in the old tub and squatting over the primitive toilet in the bathroom, which, yet to be restored, was attached to the outside of the house. I slept on a cot before the dying embers in the great stone fireplace. I was happy in a way I'd never been before. I was nearing thirty, largely uncertain of where my life was headed. Here, I was unfettered, simply at peace.

I took other vacation trips to France, but none compared with those halcyon days. Then, one morning on my way to work in Manhattan, I ran into Richard on the No. 3 subway train. He had some photographs of other properties in the area that were for sale. I moaned, seeing dreams pass before my eyes. You can do it, too, he said emphatically, and gave me the address of a French real-estate agent, who was, in fact, an Englishman. The idea hit me full force. Could I do it?

The agent sent me photographs of several properties. One with a sunny view of a little stone house in the village of Carennac utterly captivated me. Joan was in France at the time and, since she had a real-estate license, could serve as an intermediary. I could imagine her charming the French: she is an attractive blond-haired, blue-eyed woman with a sparkling personality and Southern manners. She managed to open up a personal bank account for me so that I could funnel funds from New York. Scraping every penny together, and initially splitting the cost of the house with my adventuresome older brother Gene (whose share I eventually bought), I came up with the complete payment.

That was twelve years ago. And here I am, a *propriétaire.*

Casual acquaintances find it surprising that a single woman would have a house in France. Since I have a full-time job—and a co-op, *and* two cats—in New York, I'm only able to spend a couple of weeks there twice a year. Why invest in such a remote outpost? Don't I rent it out? Renting, I respond, would not be worth the hassle. The truth, however, is that the house is a private and precious corner of myself that I'm reluctant to open up to strangers.

Close friends, on the other hand, find my owning the house perfectly understandable. They appreciate my love of France. They also know me to be a loner, a tendency that began in childhood and has continued to this day.

My father, who died just after I returned from my first European trip (a vicarious pleasure for him), suffered from severe depression, at a time and in a place where it was little understood. He was a self-created recluse, trapped, he felt, in a corporate job, with a wife, by a family, in a community to which he couldn't—or wouldn't—relate. He was a dreamer. He read mostly escapist literature: mountain-climbing and deep-sea adventures, foreign explorations, and the like. His often-reiterated message was never to settle down before seeing the world. Relationships could be snares, illusive traps, prisons. He refused to meet any of my beaux, even though I seriously dated a number of young men—they were not part of the future he held for me. I would be going to college and then to Europe, which would prepare me for a life less constrained than his.

My mother endured the stress of her marriage because she was a deeply religious person, and strongly committed to family and children. But when I approached marriageable age, she never nudged me in that direction. My two older brothers were settled and married with children. Her unspoken message to me was that there could be an equally satisfying path in life as an independent woman. I believe she found in me a ticket to the world she herself had never known. By the time I acquired the house in France, my mother was quite elderly and frail. I regret that I was never able to share it with her. She only saw my house in pictures.

I secreted the misery of my parents' life from friends. But there was a price: childhood and adolescence became an isolated, schizophrenic existence. Life within my home seemed the reality; the outside world was a shell surrounding me, false, superficial. People in that world—my school friends, most importantly—were naive, duped, ignorant of the dark side of life.

One childhood friend, Christine Lankford, was separate from all others. She lived up the block. Christine went to the public grade school and I went to Mary Queen of Peace; going, as we did, to different schools made it possible for us to create and share a private world all our own. Christine had curly strawberry-blond hair and creamy skin that picked up the rosy reflection of her hair. She was sweet-natured, unexcitable, unimaginative. I could reinvent myself in a world only the two of us shared. I could be whoever I chose with Christine, and since I had a wild imagination, this took various forms.

There was a house on our street, weathered and weed-infested, that was said to be haunted. Its real-life tenants appeared infrequently. I had decided that they were a gangster and his floozy from Los Angeles, where they were rumored to operate when they weren't in St. Louis suburbia. Indeed, the couple did have a low-life appearance, he unshaven and often shirtless, with shifty eyes that never connected with a neighborhood child's, she raven-haired and voluptuous, with dresses defining an hourglass figure and revealing bosom and calf. When they returned from their life of crime, as I imagined it, they would sit on the front steps of the house, drinking beer, defying their gentrified neighbors. They had a salivating three-legged bulldog that prowled the front yard. This cast of unsavory characters, I decided, needed a detective on the case. I began a file on the couple, describing their "history" and the precise dates and hours of their comings and goings. But this was inadequate. For important clues, it would be necessary to get inside the house. In one of their absences, I persuaded Christine to be my accomplice. While she stood faithful watch, her head jerking like a startled bird's, I threw a fist-sized rock through the window of the back door. And—how simple—we were in. Christine, a quaking sentinel, waited in the living room, where she could keep her eyes peeled on the street, while I rifled through drawers and closets. I found a cleaning bill, a movie ticket stub, a bottle of dried-up hot-pink nail polish. I pocketed them for my files. That was it. Not much to go on.

While Christine ran for home on some pressing business, I climbed the apple tree in the backyard to record our investigation in my dossier. Christine never ratted, or even referred to the incident again. I kept it to myself—and never confessed my crime to the parish priest. This was surprising, because I was always trying to dredge up some worthwhile sin for which I could be absolved.

About the best material I could come up with was on the level of lying that I'd fed the parakeet or cheating during a game of Monopoly. This "breaking and entering" was a far more serious matter, but it remained connected to a realm of fantasy.

Yet this adventure informed me about myself. I would dare what others wouldn't. I would invite rarefied experience. And, however risky, or even mistaken, I felt irreproachable.

Another encapsulated world within the real world was that of the movies. As a child, I spent hours at the cinema. Movies cast such a spell on me that I forgot who or where I was. The first film I remember was *The Wizard of Oz*, where I was taken with my Brownie troop under the supervision of our leader. Dorothy's plight was more than I could bear to watch. I crawled under the seat and cupped my palms over my ears. I was discovered—a ball of fear—when the Brownie body count at the end of the film came up with one missing.

On Saturday afternoons, all the kids went to the local movie house for a double feature. The packed, darkened house was a riot of activity: popcorn wars; constant "musical chairs" as mercurial children jockeyed allegiances, both romantic and otherwise; brawls and stampedes in the aisles. An adult wouldn't have set foot in this madhouse. The soundtrack was set at an ear-shattering level, in a futile attempt to overwhelm the noise of the live audience. Meanwhile, the screen was alive with dramatic newsreels and heart-pounding westerns and romances— inspiring subjects that were larger than ourselves. I felt swallowed up, frightened of drowning in this chaotic vortex, cowering yet content in my obscurity.

Today I prefer going to the movies by myself, when I'm

lost in the cavernous dark and surrounded by strangers. Italo Calvino captures something of this in *The Road to San Giovanni*:

> It was a time when the cinema became the world for me. A different world from the one around me, but my feeling was that only what I saw on the screen possessed the properties required of a world, the fullness, the necessity, the coherence, while away from the screen were only heterogeneous elements lumped together at random, the materials of a life, mine, which seemed to me utterly formless. The cinema as evasion, and certainly evasion was what I got out of the cinema in those years, it satisfied a need for disorientation, for the projection of my attention into a different space, a need which I believe corresponds to a primary function of our assuming our place in the world, an indispensable stage in any character formation.

Today, the movies remain a satisfying disorientation: leaving the cinema in the afternoon, as from a cocoon of perpetual night, I'm flummoxed by the daylight.

I still find great satisfaction in being in places—a town, a hotel room—aware of the fact that no one, not even close friends, knows where I am. I am free; I am uncompromised. When I left St. Louis to seek a career in New York, driving across country, I stopped at a motel in Cleveland for one night. At that moment, completely alone, whereabouts unknown, I felt finally liberated and unburdened. My father's message had taken root. My mother's spirit was with me.

When the possibility of the house in France arose, I was in my midforties. I had no ancestral ties to the country; my father's side of the family was Irish, my mother's

German. France stirred the dreamer and romantic in me. It had elegance and sophistication, the arts and high fashion, castles and royalty, cafés where literary figures whom I revered had actually sat, *haute cuisine*—in short, all that my Midwestern suburb lacked. Burdened with the childhood guilt for my parents' conflicts, I had remained at home until graduation from college. I had never had the experience of living with peers. And, though I had had my share of affairs (my first serious love came along in my junior year), I had never truly contemplated marriage. An elderly French bachelor might say, *"Je n'ai jamais trouvé ma chaussure"* (I never found my shoe), but for me it wasn't quite that simple. I wanted to avoid the trap in which I'd seen my mother. The prospect of the house came at a time in my life—settled in a job, settled in the co-op—when I was ready to turn a corner, take a plunge. Its remoteness suited me.

The *département* of the Lot, in Southwest France, is usually overlooked by guidebooks (pray that it continue, I secretly hope), which tend to focus on its westerly neighbor, the Dordogne. The Lot shares with the Dordogne the same appealing type of stone houses with red-tiled roofs and a hearty cuisine, centering on *confits* of preserved duck and goose, *foie gras*, truffles, prunes, and walnuts. Cahors is the *préfecture* of the Lot; it is also the name of the lusty "black" wine of the region. North of Cahors is the Gramat Causse, the largest *causse*, or limestone plateau, in the Quercy. It is the spot where the winding river Lot, a tributary of the Garonne, flows over rocks and loops around picturesque towns. The Dordogne River, which, in what the Michelin calls its "Quercy stretch," snakes around Carennac. The mountainous Auverge lies to the east. The Corrèze, to the north, boasts the famous china-making center of Limoges, as well as my train stop in Brive-la-Gaillarde. Because the Lot has no particular glitz—"castling," caving, and canoeing are as racy as it gets—its gentle landscape invites you to pause, rest awhile, leave behind your worries.

On my first, ecstatic journey to Carennac, I spent the first night in the *auberge* in Carennac. I was to meet the real-estate agent at the house early in the morning. It was dusk. I took a stroll through Carennac. I could have been on the moon, so far was I floating above earth. Bliss, like its opposite, grief, is strangely isolating and inexpressible; the world goes about its business at a great remove. I thought of my father, who, I'm confident, never experienced such an emotion. I recalled Evan S. Connell's Mr. Bridge, who, at church on Christmas, reflects on the word *joy*: "He asked himself if he ever had known it. If so, he could not remember. But he thought he must have known it because he understood the connotation, which would be impossible without having experienced it. However, if he had once known joy it must have been a long time ago. Satisfaction, yes, and pleasure of several sorts, and pride, and possibly a feeling which might be called 'rejoicing' after some serious worry or problem had been resolved. There were many such feelings, but none of them should be called 'joy.' He remembered enthusiasm, hope, and a kind of jubilation or exultation. Cheerfulness, yes, and joviality, and the brief gratification of sex. Gladness, too, fullness of heart, appreciation, and many other emotions. But not joy. No, that belonged to simpler minds." That would have been my father: happiness was demoted to a deceit that fools fell for. I'd believed him—in some ways, I'd been my father's child, drawn into his world of solitary darkness. Until this moment. I'd never known joy, and now I did.

The house hardly seemed a reality, but it was really

there. The bliss I felt at first mellowed over the years. And, removed from a social life that continually reinforces one's identity, I faced myself, something of a blank slate. It was a place where I could begin life almost as a child, or a brand-new person. I emerged from a cocoon and found commitment to that postcard-size patch of the world and the people who inhabited it.

Opening
a Door

1

MY HOUSE

Carennac is a fairy-tale village. From the high road it appears like a house of cards, with its jumble of cherry-red tile roofs. Its tiny meandering streets compose a story-book setting of eleventh-century church and abbey, tiny bridge, and stone houses clustered along the gently flowing Dordogne River.

Its designation as *un des plus beaux villages de France* brings excursion buses in the summer and, on Sundays, groups of families who descend on one of the local *auberges* for the traditional four-hour midday meal. There are three comfortable inns and a pint-size *alimentation*, or grocery store, owned by Monsieur Jean-Marc Coussil, a heavyset middle-aged bachelor with a sober disposition, a vivid flushed face, and eyebrows that jump with a nervous tic. Those are the only commercial enterprises. There is no café. There are virtually no permanent residents in the village, most of the houses being second homes whose owners live in more urban environments. Thus, the village feels suspended in time, nearly motionless and silent.

The church and abbey don't imperially dominate the village as is often the case in France, but are discovered nestled at an angle on a cobbled street past an inviting archway. The tympanum, sculptured in the natural stone of Carennac (*blond comme le miel*, as it is described), is surprisingly animated, with the twelve apostles conversing *tête-à-tête*. Within the church, the sixteenth-century *mise au tombeau* depicts a group of figures who must have been modeled after some local citizens, notably the Virgin, with her strong, broad peasant's face and eyes hooded in unspeakable sorrow. The adjoining cloister invites a quiet walk along its arched passageway, where it is cool on the hottest of afternoons. I always light a candle and make an irreligious wish: that Carennac will never change.

Across from a rampart overlooking the river stands a bronze bust of Fénelon (1651–1715), the renowned churchman and writer who was the senior prior of Carennac from 1681 to 1695. One of the *auberges* is named for him. His *Adventures of Télémaque*, a literary tool for his political ideas as it follows the adventures of a young man in search of his father, is said to have been written here.

A small brochure devoted to Carennac quotes Fénelon's letter to his cousin describing his entry into the town. Here is the account, in my own rough translation:

> Many personages (ecclesiastics, nobility, farmers) came from Sarlat to render homage. I walked in the majestic company of all the deputies. I arrived at the port of Carennac and beheld the platform packed with people. Two boats, full of the elite bourgeois, ad-

vanced, and at the same time I discovered that, by a
gallant strategy, the most hardened troops of this place
were hidden in a corner of the pretty island that is familiar to you. From there they assumed the order of
battle to salute me with a lot of musketry. The air was
all obscured by the fume of such a body and one could
only hear the frightening sound of saltpeter. The spirited horse that I mounted, animated by a noble ardor,
wanted to throw himself in the water, but I, more
moderate, put my foot on the earth. To the noise of the
musketry was added that of the drums.

Sarlat is an hour's drive from Carennac. Imagine the
arduous trip it must have been by horseback or carriage.
Standing by the rampart, I can gaze on Fénelon's pretty
island across the river. The troops are still hiding behind
the trees. The bronze bust of Fénelon facing the river is
softly animated, stirred by my presence. I can hear the
faint echo of the burst of gunpowder in the village, stirred
from its slumber in the sunny afternoon. There is a distant drumroll in my head.

At the crest of a hill above the village, my house sits
tucked like a bird's nest in the trees. (This is *mine*—I'm
always pinching myself.) It is invisible from the road, but
from the valley I can just spot its face. In contrast to the
normally quiet village, there is a cacophony of country
sounds about the house: the chatter of birds, the buzzing
of insects, the mooing of cows, the crowing of roosters,
and the seemingly demented skirling cries of a local female sheepherder. It is a little gem of old cream-colored
stonework and red-tiled roof, dating, according to the
real-estate agent, from the early nineteenth century. It is
called Pech Farguet. In Occitan, or the langue d'Oc, a

term used to describe the language of Southern France before the unification of the country's spoken language during the nineteenth century, it means "the hill of the little forge." In that era, a forge needed to be located as close as possible to its supply of fuel, that is to say, wood. Surrounded as it surely was by acres of pine and juniper, it would have been an ideal location to produce its weight in iron for the village of Carennac.

There is a large living room with a great fireplace occupying one wall and, opposite, long French doors open onto a tiny balcony, with a panoramic view of the valley. Through a little stone archway is a minuscule kitchen, with a half refrigerator and two-burner stove (since I market nearly every day at village *jours de marché*, these suffice). Up an angular wooden staircase is the second floor, with a small, beamed bedroom and a bath (shower, no tub). There is a garage (without a door) and a *cave*, or cellar.

Before my time, it was owned by a British architect and his wife, the Pinckneys, who did the restoration and summered there for twenty years. Now, with my arrival, I suspect that the neighbors have come to think of it as the "foreigner's place." The Pinckneys felt, for philosophic reasons, that everything should stay with the house—even Mr. Pinckney's walking stick and bird-watching binoculars. As a result, the house felt like an important legacy. Almost immediately, I wrote the Pinckneys with loads of questions. (I had never met them, since the negotiations were all done through the real-estate agent and my friend Joan. In fact, I only saw the house in photographs before making my offer.) I received a lengthy response from Mr. Pinckney, in which he described some of the features of the house:

The great table is made from three sources. The top is old floorboards, planed by me, and the best I could do. The legs were from an old house in Lymington, which I was altering, and probably date from about 1850. The footrest is made from a broken crosstree from my yacht, *Dyarchy*, built in Sweden. The chest in the salon belonged originally to my grandfather, who served in the Crimea and Indian Mutiny. The chest on the landing originally belonged to Admiral George Goldsmith, who was a great uncle of my wife, Nausicaa. The Eton bury belonged to a great uncle of mine, who was born about 1840. The small iron rack in the fireplace is intended for warming wine, and hangs on a chain which was originally used for soup.

A set of typewritten instructions about the house, entitled "Points on the Obvious and Obscure," was left in the top drawer of the bury, or oak cabinet, as I would call it. At first I read it for vital information; now I reread it for sheer amusement:

> There are two main switches in and close to the china cupboard in Galley. One is English and the other French. The French switch is on when the tumbler is up, which is the reverse of usual. When there is a thunderstorm the French one switches off automatically and has to be switched on again when the danger is past. The English one does not worry.
>
> The oven always goes out soon after lighting unless its door is left slightly open. When the oven has warmed up, its door can be shut. If a blowout occurs, it is vital to refrain from relighting until the gas has cleared, lest quite a good explosion may ensue.
>
> The fire does not like very long logs, as they seem to direct the smoke outwards. There is a small air intake

hole in the stone paving in front of the hearth with a wood plug in it. This must be opened when the fire is in use. There is a wood shield to direct the draught, which should be placed over the hole. Sometimes it is best to have the small galley window open as well. This is all vital. It can be seen from the foregoing that this fire is temperamental and has to be treated with respect or the house will be full of smoke. Replace bung in floor when you go so as to exclude mice getting in.

Altogether, I felt as if I'd fallen upon, and become the owner of, a real *character* of a house.

Initially, I followed the arrangement established by the Pinckneys, who, in their absence, always left the keys to the house with Madame Bru. Madame Bru occupied a large, uncharacteristically drab gray stucco house on the other side of the crossroad above the house. She was perhaps in her late seventies and resembled one of the chickens that ran freely about the yard: trim, if not to say scrawny, with a pointed nose and button eyes. She would scurry to the door—the *brrring* of the doorbell triggering a pitter-patter of feet, as if her visitor were long expected. She would run her rather tremulous hands through her wispy hair, as if taming ruffled feathers. Her French was relentlessly rapid-fire—"Have mercy," I wanted to plead—accompanied by quick, pecking gestures. She would sometimes give me a couple of eggs, a generous gesture since they were sustenance for herself and her family. (Once, one of her chickens was struck by a car on the road, which caused her much distress.)

Her daughter, Gabrielle, and her husband, Serge Servais, live in a beautifully restored house on adjoining property, with well-groomed gardens and lawn (the two properties were formerly owned by Gabrielle's grandparents). The Servais appear to be on the upper echelon of the social scale in "the neighborhood," judging from the interior of the house, which reflects a sophisticated taste. They met in Paris, where he worked as an industrial engineer, and lived there until his retirement. Now they prefer life in the country. Madame Servais is a petite, gracious woman, with the pert features of her mother. She always sends me home from a visit with a treat: a bag of walnuts, a bunch of strawberries, lettuce from the garden. Her husband is a large, ebullient man. He pointedly injects bits of English, which he learned long ago in school, into conversations with me. He is hard of hearing and tends, particularly when trying out an English phrase, to shout. "OW DOO YOU DOO?" He's a punster as well. When I asked them if they'd known the Pinckneys, he replied, "The Pickles? *Les Cornichon? Non.*" They had been living in Paris then.

Two years after I moved into my house, Madame Bru's health began to fail. She was taken to a rest home and left my keys with the Bézamats, a family I was acquainted with who lived down the road. As delicately as possible, I explained to the Bézamats that I had become concerned about Madame being in charge of the keys, since she had become so feeble, and though she was expected to return from the home, I asked if they would assume the responsibility. Madame Bru never did return—she died in the rest home eight years ago—so now the keys are run back and forth to the Bézamats.

Madame Fernande Bézamat was first enlisted by the real-estate agent to clean the house prior to my arrival, and she has continued to do so ever since (I just write her several weeks ahead). She seems to appreciate the extra spending money. Her price is nearly as much as what I pay the young male linguist student who cleans for me in New York, but the steadfast attention the Bézamats give to the house the rest of the year is invaluable. In the fall, after the house has been closed during the long hot summer, she leaves a plastic bag the size of a basketball in the garage, filled with the flies *(mouches)* she's swept up.

Madame appears solid and strong-minded. She is twenty-four years younger than her husband, who is seventy, though she's not the least bit deferential toward him. A mild neurological condition causes her head to twitch slightly, a movement that punctuates her conversation. She has a weathered complexion from working from sunup to sundown over long stretches for local entrepreneurs, gathering asparagus, strawberries, and walnuts in their respective seasons. In the fall, the walnuts leave her hands stained a deep mahogany for months. Not long ago, she had to have a knee operation due to a loss of cartilage; the doctor said she'd spent too much time on her knees. I long to bring out some humor in her, to break the tedium of her life, and she is quick to laugh. Once, I found her sitting on the landing of her house with her dog, Bobbie (pronounced with a long O), a friendly gray-and-white mutt. She explained that Bobbie was in an agitated state because a neighboring female dog was in heat. *"C'est dûr d'être amoureux,"* I said in mock sympathy. She thought this was uproarious, to attribute a natural animal instinct to a human emotion. But there was a harsh ring in her laughter, implying, I thought, a skepticism about romance.

Monsieur must have been a handsome young man; he still is handsome, with vestiges of a zesty sensuality in his teasing eyes. Though he has a heart condition, his sharp, clear features are unmarred by age. He uses the name Marius for any official, written matter, but is called Charles by his wife and friends. I have asked him how he met his wife. He simply replied, à la George Leigh Mallory when speaking of Mount Everest, *"Elle n'était pas loin"* (she wasn't far). So much for my notions of the romantic French.

The Bézamats have a sizable vegetable garden, large enough to provide for the family. Monsieur Bézamat was a *cultivateur*, as was his father before him, for nearly thirty years, and then a *maçon tailleur enpérre* (stone mason), taking only those jobs that suited him. He is always obliging, if not anxious, to do any odd jobs around my house for a little extra money. As soon as I arrive, he is quick to point out whatever needs fixing: a broken hinge, weathered paint, a leak in the roof. He tallies figures according to the *ancien* system, which went out long ago with De Gaulle. It's *d'habitude.* His wife scoffs at this sign of stubbornness or unadaptability, but I can understand. It makes things more sensible to him. Wouldn't it be shocking to find that something worth, say, a hundred dollars costs only a dollar?

The Bézamats have four children. I first met Serge, the eldest son, when he was in his late teens. He lives at home and works in the wood business. Colette, two years younger, works in Brive, a bustling town with a big market and cathedral about an hour's drive away; I have never met her and wondered why to my knowledge she never visits home. Kati and Françoise, twins, were born after a ten-year gap. From the first, I saw that they were poles apart. Françoise was reserved and diffident, striving for independence and womanhood. Kati was rambunctious and outgoing, a scamp and tomboy who was still having fun being a child. It was always Kati who, out of an innate curiosity, tagged along with her parents when they came to the house, and rolled around with Bobbie on the grass while her parents and I went about our business.

There is, and I imagine there will always be, only one set of keys. They are an irregular mix, to an outer and inner front door and the *cave*. The key to the *cave* is a gigantic, old iron piece that resembles the turnkey to a castle. Yet, over all these years of passing them back and forth, they've never been misplaced or lost. The keys constitute an unbroken link in our relationship.

Without the Bézamats, I often think, how would I survive?

2

MY NEIGHBORS

During my first fall at Pech Farguet in 1984, I became acquainted with the Hirondes. When I needed firewood, Monsieur Bézamat informed me that Raymond Hironde was the man to see. Monsieur Hironde and his wife, Simone, live in Magnagues (pronounced something like maan-yag-ge, a word that always feels like peanut butter sticking to the roof of my mouth). It is only a five-minute walk up the road from my house. It's a mere hamlet with a few dozen houses and a small square, where an annual fête is held in July. There is a defunct church and beside it the *presbytère*, which has a story behind it that Monsieur Hironde hastened to tell me. In 1944, the Normandy invasion had taken place, but "the war was not yet over." Two British officers landed in parachutes near Miers—there's a marker designating the spot. One of the men, Major George Hiller, had been shot by the SS. The locals discovered him and hid him in the *presbytère* in

Magnagues. There he was cared for by a doctor from nearby Vayrac and an English nurse. After the war, the nurse and the major married. He was much older and died years ago, but she still comes to the *presbytère*, which they'd bought and made their home after the church was closed. There is a plaque to the left of the door that reads: ICI FUT SOIGNÉ GEORGE HILLER MAJOR BRITTANIQUE AUPRÈS DES GROUPES VÉNY, BLESSÉ PAR LE SS EN JUILLET 1944 (here, the British major George Hiller with the Vény group, wounded by the SS in July 1944, was cared for).

Monsieur Hironde is an avuncular gentleman, with a gurgling laugh that starts deep in his throat and erupts in a snort through his nose. A natural-born teacher, he is a storehouse of facts and figures—the depths of chasms, heights of mountains, historical data, that sort of thing. And he speaks slowly and exactingly to me—though with a pronounced, endearing lisp—as if he were addressing, well, a foreigner. I don't regard this as the least condescending, but rather as a sign of perceptiveness, an ability to recognize my need. (I have given up pleading with the Bézamats to speak more slowly.)

He said he could readily supply me with wood. The very next afternoon he arrived with a tractorload of logs of various thicknesses, cut to fit my fireplace. There had been no discussion of the amount; he had simply cut down a tree. He dumped the logs in a great heap outside the house. I paid him for the firewood and hoisted two logs under either arm. It was going to be a day's work, carrying them piecemeal down the flight of stone steps to the *cave*. He stood rooted in place, looking conflicted. Then, with a generosity of spirit from which I would benefit for years and an *allez-y*, he picked up an armload himself, balancing the bundle as if he were cradling a baby, and paraded after me to the *cave*. We passed back and forth, like soldiers, up and back, up and back. In the end, the *cave* held a tidy, mountainous stack of logs, a supply for many winters to come. I was deeply satisfied with this physical exploit. That night I would have a glass of wine in front of a roaring fire.

Monsieur Hironde, I eventually learned, was retired from his position as a middleman in the mushroom industry (an *agriculteur*), employed by the Boy-Maury factory located in nearby Biars-St-Céré. During the mushroom season in the fall, he would travel approximately two hundred kilometers a day to a dozen collection points where pickers amassed the harvest. He would pay the harvesters, and in turn, the factory would pay him. In a good year, he would earn perhaps twenty thousand francs—all in the course of several months. On the side, he also supplied wood.

He lives in a house built by his grandparents in 1912. When his parents married in 1914, they moved to the house, where Raymond was born in 1922. When he married his first wife in 1950, they lived with their parents in the house. Raymond and his first wife had five children.

Simone was born in Carennac in 1922 and married her first husband in 1941. They had four children. When both Raymond and Simone's spouses died, they married in 1984. That was the year I met them, though at the time I assumed they were a longtime married couple. They'd known each other since childhood, which goes a long way toward explaining their obvious compatibility.

Whenever I stop by their house, the Hirondes invite me in for a coffee or a glass of Monsieur's homemade prune *eau de vie*, even in the late morning—despite the rumored French reluctance to welcome foreigners into their homes. Over the years we have graduated to using first names with each other. The ice was broken when Madame Hironde sent me a Christmas card signed "Simone and Raymond." Subsequently—I can't recall the specific occasion—she addressed me by my first name. I warmed as if she'd physically touched me. After that I gingerly tried out "Simone" and "Raymond"—lyrical to my ears—which caused no tremors. So we were established on a more intimate basis, though we've never gone so far as to *tutoyer* each other.

When I visit, we sit in the small, spartan dining room, furnished simply with a wooden chest for dishes and a plain wooden table and chairs within the hand-warming vicinity of a small fireplace. The adjoining kitchen has sparkling white walls and tile. There is a third room on this floor, a study across the front hall, with an astonishingly ostentatious *armoire* that Simone proudly points out as a family heirloom. Otherwise, there is not a picture or photograph, decorative object or bibelot adorning any of the rooms. The Hirondes are not impoverished. They're just clutter-free, detached from material goods. Yet where is their sense of nostalgia, their taste or fancy? Without clues or context, they seem ill-defined. I feel, selfishly, that something is being withheld from me.

We talk of travel (they have been to Portugal, Spain, Hungary, countries that are among the more affordable vacation spots), politics (which, given the complexity of the subject and Raymond's excitability when roused by an issue, often leaves me in the dust), family matters, and, often, at my instigation, food and cooking. They are rarely prompted to inquire about my life in New York, which must seem terribly remote. It's more natural to talk about our immediate world.

Raymond warms to the role of raconteur, especially after some *eau de vie*. In fact, he looks something like a vaudevillian, with slick brown hair parted on one side and naturally uplifted eyebrows that give him an air of perpetual surprise. Simone sits somewhat formally beside him, sometimes with the distracted air of one who has heard all this before. He is fond of recounting a story about the first time he left his homeland, as a soldier during the war. In the prologue, he explains his strict Catholic background, his sole experience with the priesthood. The main story recounts his service in Hungary, and his first attempt to attend church there. To his utter shock, the priest arrived with a wife on one arm and a child in tow. A blatant flaunting of sin! Then, enlightenment: this was a Protestant church! Everything was put to rights: one man's sin was another's virtue. As he retold this tale, flushed and full of good cheer, his laughter would cause his head to tip back in merriment.

Simone, in contrast to his unfailing jolliness, has a sensitive, selfless temperament. Although I have seen her grow animated when talking about a travel adventure or anticipating a visit with friends, she is more often focused on problems of family or friends. On one of my visits, she wept openly over the recent, premature loss of a daughter-in-law, who left behind young children. A sturdy-looking woman—though she is troubled by bronchitis—she has a tidy, fastidious manner, habitually attired in a crisp belted dress in warm weather and a plain woolen dress and sweater in the cold. Her silvery blue hair always appears freshly coiffed (early one morning, she greeted me in a bathrobe with her hair in tight little rollers, and on several occasions I've encountered her on the way to the hairdresser). Simone is a familiar type of person to me—not unlike the Midwestern women I grew up with—down-to-earth, religious, family-oriented, without airs. I'm always at ease in her company.

Five years ago I discovered a surprising aspect of the Hirondes' relationship. I had stopped by their house to see if Monsieur could come over to trim the lawn. He promised to come over that afternoon. He would be leaving later, he said, to fetch Simone—*mon compagnon*, he called her—who was taking a cure in the Pyrenees for a bout of arthritis. *Mon compagnon!* The words—not *ma femme*—jumped out of the sentence and gave me a jolt.

All this time I had thought they were married. Perhaps that had only been a polite way of signifying their union in 1984. Still, why should I be shocked? Obviously, I had stereotyped them as a straitlaced, traditional country couple, whose living together out of wedlock would be unacceptable to family and neighbors. But I was also a little put out. The Hirondes, who were so protective of me, had become something of parental figures. The child in me surfaced; this felt like a small betrayal.

That same spring of 1991, Simone proposed that the two of us take an excursion to the property her *petit-cousin*, Jean-François Fraysse, was restoring. This was something I must see. This distant relative, she said, lived most of the year in New York, while his seventy-year-old uncle, Georges Fraysse, did the lion's share of the labor.

The place was only a mile away. When we arrived we found the elder Fraysse on his hands and knees, planting shoots of lavender. A stocky figure, he had a ruddy moon-shaped face with a picket fence of grayish teeth, bushy eyebrows, and a shock of flyaway white hair. He stood to greet me, with the agility of a twenty-year-old. Etiquette requires a Frenchman with soiled hands to avoid a gritty handshake with a woman. Yet, not to appear unwelcoming, he may extend a bent wrist—or, if that's soiled as well, an elbow to be shaken instead. I shook Monsieur Fraysse's elbow.

The vast property, Simone said as he led us to the main house, included approximately fifty hectares, or a hundred and twenty-five acres, as I later calculated, and had been in the family for three generations. Monsieur Georges Fraysse had already cleared an expanse on the highest hill behind the house where he had planted three hundred chestnut trees. On the far side of the house was a magnificent grange in the ubiquitous stone and red tile, and on the other side an enormous beehive of a *four à pain*, or woodburning bread oven, which would be restored to working order.

When we entered the house, I could see that this was no ordinary undertaking. The structure was little more than a bare skeleton of roof and walls, the dirt floor covered by rickety wood planks. The best-preserved feature was a walk-in fireplace where the cooking would have been done in the past (in fact, there were some old iron cooking pots gathering dust on the hearth for which I, or a New York City antiques dealer, would have given a pretty penny).

I asked Monsieur Fraysse how long he thought the restoration would take. He shrugged his shoulders with an *"ah, ben,"* not in a sense of defeat but as if to say that things like this have a way of unfolding in their own time.

At the end of our brief tour of the house, Simone said she had something to show me. She prodded Monsieur Fraysse into rummaging through a cluttered drawer of an old wooden chest. Eventually, he produced a single sheet of heavy paper. On one side was a reproduction of a photograph depicting a once-familiar rural scene in this part of France—a farmhouse with a young *paysan* leading a team of oxen to the fields. On the other side was a menu, with the name La Luncheonette scrolled across the top. Her *petit-cousin*, Simone announced, was the chef and owner of this restaurant in Manhattan.

I studied the small selection of classic French dishes, momentarily mystified. At the bottom of the menu was the restaurant's fringe, if not to say seedy, address on Tenth Avenue, along with the phone number—proof to me that it did, in fact, exist. Standing on the wobbly floorboards, I squinted my eyes to imagine a French restaurant on Tenth Avenue, owned by a cousin of Simone's. It was so improbable, a thread connecting here to there.

Simone didn't suggest that I look him up, but I immediately made a resolution to do so.

Back in New York, I stopped in for an early dinner. The entrance to the place was on Eighteenth Street. The intersection is at the heart of a desolate stretch of warehouses. The view through the lace-curtained window is the parking lot of a truck-leasing operation. Hardly the setting for a *pâté de lapin* and *cervelles au beurre noir,* which is what I ordered.

I asked the young waitress if Jean-François was free for a moment. He emerged from the kitchen, a man in his midforties, who, I could see, might in old age resemble his uncle Georges. I explained that we were something of neighbors *(voisins)* in France. He collapsed in disbelief into the chair across from me. I finger-drew a small map on the tablecloth, the roads leading from my house to his. His face softened into a broad smile. He knew precisely my little road—a mere hairline on the most detailed map of the region. When I asked him when he would be going back to France, his face clouded. The work of the restaurant took up all his time. Was he worrying if it would survive? I wondered. Then his face brightened, as if he had been transported a world away. He raised cupped hands, as if testing for raindrops, and said that as his house there was undergoing restoration and was at the moment roofless, it was like being on a continual *pique-nique*.

He returned to the kitchen. I lingered over my *tarte tatin*, still warm from the oven, and coffee. I was overcome with a disturbing and unpleasant sense of dislocation. For a moment that intimate, closed world of Pech Farguet had taken root on unsavory Tenth Avenue. It didn't belong here. It was diminished, unappreciated in these surroundings. I wanted to lock up La Luncheonette and throw the key away.

In the fall, as soon as I settled in the house, I walked the short distance to the Hirondes. The little road cuts a swathe over the high hill. You're at the top of the world. The meandering, glittering river coils like a loose bracelet in the valley. Sheep grazing in a lower pasture are immobile, like ceramic figures in a crèche scene. The piercing shrieks of the woman driving her cows home on the lower road puncture the air like gunshots.

The trees were just beginning to show hints of gold; the full glory of fall doesn't arrive in the Lot until late October or early November. The air was so cool that I quickened my pace, feeling the tug in the muscles at the backs of my legs. I was exhilarated, feeling victorious. My meeting with Jean-François was a little trophy that could forge a closer bond with the Hirondes.

Simone opened the door and motioned me into the dining room with her usual warm greeting—unsurprised, as if I'd been there just yesterday. We sat on two stiff wooden chairs before the fire. I told her straightaway about my meeting with her *petit-cousin*, ending with the treat of the wonderful *tarte tatin*. That, she said, beaming, was probably her recipe. Or, she amended, the family recipe. I patted my stomach, as if I was still digesting the last bite, and waxed on about the light crust, the warmth of the apples contrasting with the coolness of the whipped cream.

Would I like the recipe? Simone asked. She knew it by heart, the way she knew most of what she cooked. To three cups of flour . . . she began her recital. I listened contentedly. I knew I'd never be able to equal that *tarte tatin*. I wouldn't even attempt it. It was her confiding the recipe that counted.

3

MY FIRST GUESTS
(i.e., Jean and the Bats)

My first houseguest was Jean Breton, a former lover, who, despite the dissolution of our romance, has remained a close friend. In our romantic days, before my acquisition of the house, we had taken a number of vacations together in France: to Provence, Alsace, the Basque country. Jean's family is French-Canadian and he grew up speaking French at home. In France, people were sometimes baffled by his accent. Despite this, his ease in the language has always been a source of envy to me, although he has no comprehension of the rules of grammar and, to my amusement, cannot recite the alphabet phonetically. If something complicated needed saying in our travels, I relied on him. If something needed spelling (a far less frequent occurrence, of course), he relied on me.

Jean liked to travel in style, so we frequently stayed in plush country inns or châteaus. He is ten years older than I and worked his way up from the position of clerk to the president of a bank in Connecticut, where he lives. He could afford luxurious travels—and I couldn't have been happier to be the beneficiary. Yet Jean is not pretentious. We have also stayed in some second-rate and offbeat places, and he can roll with the punches. Traveling with another person is a supreme test of compatibility: it's not only a matter of shared interests, but of pace. Jean and I are completely in sync: quick to be ready to go at the same time, flagging and seeking a break simultaneously, identical in our attention spans. We also agree on the critical matter of baggage: one piece of luggage is the limit. That means reappearing in the same outfit, but who cares? No one but ourselves would see our clothes tomorrow.

Jean was thrilled at my acquisition of the house, and the following year he responded enthusiastically to an invitation to spend a week in the spring. I spent several days at the house before his arrival, obsessing over the possible combinations and permutations of excursions and menus. I picked him up at the train station in Brive.

The first day we marketed in a local village—Jean and I share a love of cooking—and that evening had a golden roasted chicken stuffed with rosemary from the bush in the yard and a whole head of lavender garlic; tiny sautéed potatoes that tasted as if they'd just been plucked from the earth; coarse, crusty *pain de compagne*; and a big green salad. For wine, we had a buttery Meursault I'd been saving for a special occasion (Jean is a wine connoisseur), and for dessert, a specialty of the region: an apple tart with furls of pastry as thin and crisp as parchment, flavored with an *eau de vie de prune*. After the fire was reduced to glowing embers—in early spring, there is a

chill in the air after the sun goes down—we climbed the
stairs for bed.

There is only a double bed in the tiny upstairs bedroom, but neither of us felt awkward about sleeping side
by side. Former passion is similar to vanished pain: a fact
remembered but no longer felt. We burrowed under the
covers and turned off the light, with the distant hooting
of an owl—why is it always only a single owl?—an invitation to dream.

In the middle of the night, we were abruptly awakened
by the most alarming sounds. They emanated from the
other side of the wall by the headboard: a frantic scratch-
ing, sounding like the fingernails of a thousand skeletons
clawing their way from their graves, accompanied by
faint, poignant cries, the whimperings of monster babies.
We bolted upright and grappled for the light switch.

"Bats," Jean pronounced. I was aghast but believed
him—he'd grown up in the country, and spent summers
on his grandparents' farm in Canada. "Only a nuisance,"
he added, now that he'd gotten a grip on himself.

His words had the opposite of the soothing effect he
intended. "Bats!" I shrieked, tunneling under the covers,
as if they would swoop through the window in a hellish
swarm.

Jean pounded on the wall with his fist. *"Taisez-vous!"*
he shouted, commanding quiet with mock ferociousness.

And sure enough, there was a sudden, blessed silence.
It was a relief, but far from reassuring. Jean switched off
the light, slid under the covers, and hardly missing a beat,
was soon breathing deeply in sleep. I lay staring into the
dark; the wicked, jagged-winged creatures, their eyes
an iridescent green, soared through the nighttime of
my mind.

And then it began all over again: the incessant scratch-
ing, the hideous faint wails, what I now picked up as the
ghostly rustling of wings. I nudged Jean, who was, of
course, already awake.

"What can we *do?*" I anguished. Without a word, he
bounded out of bed, trundled down the stairs, and reappeared with a broom clutched in one hand like a sword.
Jean, who is a small, wiry man, an eleven-time mara-
thoner, stood rockily on the bed beside my head in his
candy-striped pajama shorts. I released my locked arms
and grasped the ankles of his bantam, muscular legs to
lend support.

The bats had hushed at the first few blows, but Jean
continued to pound determinedly on the wall. This was
overkill, I thought grumpily. But suddenly there was a
great swooshing sound, like a flock of birds flushed from
a field by hunters. I peered out the window at the starry,
moonlit sky, expecting it to be darkened by a thousand
bats—the stuff of comic books.

"They're gone," Jean said with a deep sigh, dropping
to his knees like a penitent. He tossed the broom to the
floor and switched off the light. We rolled over on our
stomachs, each facing the outside of the bed but clasping
hands between us, like children after a bad dream.

Jean's enthusiasm to see my part of France was bound-
less. We took one day trip after the next, visiting the castles and caves that are a particular fascination of the Lot.
While the region contains more famous and impressive
castles, such as Castelnaud, my favorite is Montal, which
I regard as my neighborhood castle since it's a mere
fifteen-minute drive away. Castles are called *châteaux*,

meaning either a certifiable fortified castle or simply a grand country home. In fact, Montal is not a castle per se, but a *manoir de plaisance*, built by Jeanne de Balsac d'Entraygues, the widow of the governor of the Haute-Auvergne, in 1523. It's not ostentatious—you can truly imagine daily life being lived there—but it does have an impressive fireplace in the second-floor dining room with an astonishing life-size stone stag, and a unique staircase, which winds around a central wall, and whose underside, carved with shells and fantastic birds, is visible from below as you mount the stairs.

The tour guide at Montal had us both riveted. He was a young man with a startling mien. It's as if someone had taken his head and given it a hard upward thrust on one side, rendering his features at a slant: the eyebrow and eye higher on the right, the nose skewed, the mouth pulled down on the left, the jaw overshot. Yet he wasn't unattractive. He had a boyish look and an eagerness that is typical of young tour guides in France. They speak with a practiced clarity, for which I am always grateful (subjects such as Aubusson tapestries presenting something of a challenge to the nonnative speaker). And there's something of the actor in them: how else can they deliver the same material over and over again with unfeigned delight, surprise, and gravity. (Possibly France's aspiring actors work as tour guides, as opposed to those in New York, who work as waiters and waitresses.)

Jean found the story of Montal as heartrending as I had on my first visit. The brief entry in the Michelin calls it *"un miracle d'amour maternel."* It was built by Madame d'Entraygues for her son Robert, who was fighting in Italy in the service of François I. All was made ready to welcome home the proud soldier. But, tragically, only the

dead body of Robert, who had been killed in battle, returned. The château stands as poignant testimony to her
love: an ornate letter *R* can be seen in the exterior frieze
of the courtyard. She blocked up the tower window
where she had stood watch for the return of her son and
had carved beneath it the words PLUS D'ESPOIR. No more
hope. The guide notes that the statue of a young boy
above one of the courtyard windows was decapitated by
Madame. *"On pense,"* he says—so it is supposed—and
Michelin does not document the fact. A second son, who
was a church dignitary, was relieved of his ecclesiastical
duties after his brother's death so that the family line
could continue. And continue it did—this son sired nine
children.

This is as far as the records go. But what next? I
wanted to know. How did Madame d'Entraygues deal
with her grief? Did she pine away at Montal? Abandon it
in order to seek the solace of her family? A widow at that
time—surely not an uncommon state, given the ravages of
battle and disease—must have faced enormous hardship
in her unwelcome independent state. Yet she survived to
the ripe old age of ninety-two, outliving both sons.

Since Jean and I are both walkers, we spent some time
merely strolling about nearby villages. One day we
stopped in a small village, whose only point of interest
was its church. I cannot resist popping into any church.

All the villages around my house, as in France in general, have cross-shaped signs posted at the village limit,
listing the hour (or hours) of the Sunday Mass. Yet despite the church's effort to modernize its services (French
replacing Latin, folk music on guitar replacing the Grego-
rian chant), the congregation at local Masses is usually a
tiny band—typically two dozen women in their sixties, a

handful of men the same age, the rare family—their negligible numbers further diminished by the enormity of the
edifice, which renders their feeble, rote prayers unintelligi-
ble, and their eggshell-thin voices raised in song pathetic.

Jean is highly principled but skeptical about organized
religion. We go our separate ways at churches, which I
imagine he sees as temples of questionable authority in a
faith he cannot hold. He happily set off to scour up a restaurant for lunch.

In fact, I'm not stirred by any religious fervor but
rather in thrall to the past (a past that is so *present* in
France). The most remote village church can possess its
own monumentality and grandeur, although it may be
gaudily, even tackily appointed. I am as impressed, at
times, by these outposts as I am by the grand Gothic
cathedrals of major cities (Paris, of course, as well as
Chartres, Bourges, Reims, Amiens). These country cous-
ins are stout testimony to the devotion and dedication of
the faithful.

On my first exploration of the countryside, I had
driven to Collonges-la-Rouge, an unusual nearby village
whose name is derived from the houses and streets that
glow with a red hue from the indigenous clay from which
they're constructed. I happened on a stonemason at work
atop a tall ladder, restoring the frieze of the little church
in the square. It was late morning, sunny and hushed.
Transfixed, I watched him at work until it was time for
lunch. The ancient sound of metal chipping away at
stone, a ritualistic and patient *thung, thung, thung,* was
mesmerizing. Nothing, apparently, has changed since the
Middle Ages in this time-honored craft.

* * *

While Jean wandered on this particularly gray and drizzly day, I stood in the ponderous Romanesque interior, arms wrapped around myself in the stony coldness, slowly pirouetting. It is another satisfaction in visiting country churches outside of the hours of service to find yourself utterly alone, as I did then. The pulpit, an ornately carved wooden shell, stood empty; the tall candles flickered in the cold breaths of air; the eyes of saints stared benignly into space, as if they were looking at something no longer there. I smelled a trace of incense, which triggered a response in me that was similar to Proust's madeleines. I felt a benediction, a gentle recollection of childhood naïveté. I no longer pray; but for a moment I experienced the warm spiritual presence of my mother.

Jean was jumping in place and flapping his arms on this bone-chilling day like a kid making an angel in the snow. A stroll required more grit than we cared to muster. It was noon, a little early for lunch for the two of us—though not for the French, who break from noon to two or three in the afternoon for their midday repast. Nonetheless, we sought the comfort of the indoors. Rather than drive on, we scurried across the square to what Jean had found to be the only restaurant in the village. As we entered the tiny dining room, we were engulfed by its steamy warmth and the smoky aromas of grilled meat. There were perhaps a dozen tables, all occupied save one—waiting, it seemed, just for us. The locals, mainly men, were a spirited bunch, regaling each other over trencher-size platters of food. We had a restorative lunch of soup, sizzling steak, and slender, crisp french fries. Would we like dessert? the sole, matronly waitress asked, between her breathless whirling-dervish rounds. Jean, who could leave no stone unturned, ordered a dish of home-made prune ice cream—prunes, a speciality of the region, turn up in everything from a pork stew to *eau de vie*. I watched as he slipped a teaspoonful into his mouth. The expression on his face was that of a saint's in a medieval religious painting, eyes rolling heavenward in a swoon.

Besides bountiful lunches in local restaurants, we shared a picnic on a grassy hill overlooking the Dordogne River, and dinners at the house prepared with the best of the local markets. The days seemed long and short at the same time, and then they were gone. It was time for Jean's departure. He had decided to take a plane from Bordeaux instead of repeating the train ride back to Paris. I gladly agreed to drive him to the airport, a three-hour trip. We could see a little of the wine country and enjoy dinner and an overnight stay in the town (neither of us had been to Bordeaux).

After breakfast we set off. Just outside of St-Emilion we stopped at a winery and then ambled around the town. On one of our first trips together, Jean had suc-cumbed to what proved to be the folly of purchasing a case of very expensive wine. He had stashed it in the trunk of the car, but it had been a constant concern. It was summer, and he worried that if we parked in a sunny spot, the wine would be ruined. In an effort to keep it at a relatively stable temperature, we would often drive round and round towns searching for a shady spot. It was like traveling with a sick passenger. After that, he decided, sensibly, not to purchase any more wine to bring home. But that didn't prevent him from looking.

We had lunch at the elegant Plaisance, near the cathe-dral in St-Emilion and, at our leisurely pace, didn't arrive in Bordeaux until midafternoon. Since it was off-season, we hadn't thought it necessary to make a hotel reservation. Jean was behind the wheel and I cracked the handy Michelin. We started with hotels in the *grand comfort* category (the Frantel). Jean pulled up in front and double-parked while I bounded in to make a reservation. There were no rooms available. We went down a notch to *très comfortable* (the Terminus). Full up. The Normandie. Full. The Majestic. Full. *De bon comfort* (the Royal Médoc). Booked.

This was unheard of. I asked the desk clerk at the Royal why the hotels were all full. The town, he informed me, had been turned inside out for a *fête de musique*. The arch of his eyebrows and the wagging of his index finger—a sort of reprimand—implied that an attempt to find a room was futile. I trotted back to the car and reported this to Jean. Moving on to *simple mais convenable*, we struck out at the Centre and Trianon. The Michelin list was now exhausted. *I* was exhausted, tired of bounding in and out of the car. It was now approaching six o'clock. A niggling panic and incipient shortness of temper were just under the surface between us. The point now was to get a room, any room. After making several random stops at hotels that were also full, we turned a corner and stumbled on one that had a distinctly old-world, if not to say decrepit, appearance.

I heaved with my shoulder in an effort to budge the heavy oak door and adjusted my eyes to the dim interior. Pale, dusty streams of light from a filmy skylight revealed a weathered, unattended reception desk. A tiny lamp with a frayed green silk shade cast a yellow circle of light on a leather ledger. A brass bell sat beside it. I gave it a sharp ring with the palm of my hand. I heard the drone of a television, the creaking of a chair, and the slow scuf-

fling of slippered feet from beyond a shut door at the end
of the hallway. The door slowly opened and an imposing
woman came forward. Perhaps in her sixties, she was
dressed in a long black skirt, to which she gave a Loretta
Young–type swish, a black sweater cut low to reveal scallops of freckled bosom, with a large egg-shaped yellow
pendant nestled in the cleavage, and a black shawl and
turban with glittering gold threads. There was, however,
a mothball air about her; she struck me as a woman who
had fallen on hard times, yet still strove to create an impression of elegance. She had an overbite and deep paren-
thetical creases enclosing her crimson mouth; her face had
the hardness of a ventriloquist's dummy. In her right arm
she supported an enormous cat resembling a Siamese, but
tailless, which she placed ceremoniously on the desk. The
cat ducked its head to rub against my shoulder. "Mignon," she said approvingly to the cat, in a startlingly
husky voice. She stroked it with arthritic fingers, poignant
in a woman so obviously concerned with beauty.

"*Oui,*" she said, drawing out her response like a whistle, when she heard my travails. She had a room! I rose
on the toes of my feet and clapped for joy. I explained
that I would run out and inform my friend, who would
park the car. And how much was the room? Twenty dollars. This was amazingly cheap. Why? a little patrolman
in my brain questioned. She required the money on the
spot. I plunked down the cash, and she handed me the
keys. There was no mention of breakfast.

That was the last I saw of her. Jean and I found our
room down the hallway on the first floor. The long,
skinny key slid up to its neck in the door lock and turned
loosely over and over without effect. We took turns:
"Here, let me," "Let me." Eventually, by moving it a

gradual notch forward, like a thief cracking a safe, Jean got it to catch hold.

The room was enormous. In fact, it had all the features of a miniature house. To the left of the door was a knee-high double bed, covered with an orange comforter and the type of long sausage-shaped pillow, as resistant as a punching bag, which is common to French hotels. The mattress was bound to be soft and lumpy, the cover revealing hills and valleys. Beside the bed was a tiny table and a lamp with a fluted plastic shade. This constituted the bedroom. The vast middle portion of the room served as living room, with two stiff, offputting love seats separated by a faux marble table topped with a vase of dusty plastic flowers. There were no windows, but heavy, ceiling-to-floor drapes hanging on a portion of the "living room" wall opened to reveal an air shaft, brightly lit like a stage set, as if to simulate sunlight.

At the far end of the room, to the left, was the kitchen, with a mini-refrigerator and a small square wooden table. The bathroom, to the right, separated by a Japanese-style room divider, had a miniature sink with a glass shelf that would hold exactly one toothbrush and a tube of toothpaste, and, above it, a cloudy mirror. The shower was a sort of plastic stall fitted into the corner.

There were no luggage stands to distract from the impression of home. A single closet contained three plastic hangers. After silently surveying the capacious, if shabby, surroundings, Jean and I hastily unpacked the barest necessities.

Mignon—either the cat's name or a term of endearment—had managed to slip into the room on our heels and had taken up a post on one of the love seats, adding a further note of domesticity. Jean was arranging his shaving kit on the kitchen table. Fond as he is of cats, he experiences an immediate allergic reaction in their presence. His eyes were already tearing. I sidled up to Mignon nonchalantly—with that just-whistling-a-happy-tune posture to prevent her bolting. Surprisingly, she crawled into my arms, purring in contentment. When I promptly tossed her out the door, she glanced back, miffed.

Jean and I were famished. We splashed cool water on our faces and were ready to go. After a casual dinner at a local restaurant, we dropped into bed—or rather, we sank into the bowels of the mattress, glued back-to-back. Jean had an early-morning flight. Neither of us slept well. Throughout the night, our sleep was disturbed by an annoyingly slow-motion opening and closing of doors in the hallway, the tumbling of keys in locks, the hushed traffic of feet on creaking floorboards.

That was Bordeaux.

Driving back to the house, I was both savoring the pleasure of Jean's visit and feeling *un trou* in my chest at his sudden absence. Reviewing our days together, I had a sudden insight. Jean and I had stayed in a brothel.

It all fell into place: the room, the footsteps in the night, Madame's appearance. I tittered. This was rich; my mind seized on the possibilities. Madame could once have been a stage actress who, in her middle years, had fallen on hard times. Perhaps she had had many lovers in her life, but all had deserted her, so that she was left to fend for herself. She had established a "house," I concluded, of beautiful young prostitutes, all of whom adored her as their own mother. Her loyal clientele included a local banker, a classy restaurateur, a Parisian businessman, who held her in strictest confidence. It was, so, well, *French*.

But why had she given us the room? Was it my helplessness and desperation? I rather doubted it. Probably it was nothing more than a bird in hand. The room was going empty that night—and twenty bucks is twenty bucks.

The idea of staying in a house of ill-repute was immensely satisfying. That would shock the nuns who had supervised my strict Catholic upbringing. "Ha!" I erupted unwittingly in the stillness of the car. "Ha!"

"N'ayez pas peur," Monsieur Bézamat said, when I told him about the bats. *"Pas méchantes."* These were phrases—"don't be afraid, "they're not vicious"—I would hear repeated many times. He led me into the house and produced a large, coffee-table-type book—or perhaps it was a children's book—devoted to the *animaux de France,* with large, bright-colored illustrations accompanied by brief text. It took a while for him to find what he was looking for. Monsieur Bézamat is obviously in dire need of eyeglasses—he holds a book at an unnatural distance and peers at it down his nose through shuttered eyes—yet he resists wearing them unless they are forced upon him by his wife. He finally opened to a page with an illustration of a black bat—looking a bit *méchant,* actually. Thus, I learned the word for bat—*chauve-souris*— which, indeed, had a nonthreatening, if not to say, tender, sound to it.

Monsieur explained that because the house was left unoccupied for long stretches of time, animals would hole up and hibernate there. I had a Technicolor fantasy of all manner of little creatures huddled together for warmth in the microscopic Disneyland of my house.

Later, at home in New York, I read a piece in *The New*

Yorker about bats. Monsieur Bézamat had been absolutely correct in portraying them as harmless. The article related that bats are the unlucky recipients of a bad press, which paints them as evil and ominous. I recalled a horrifying falsehood from my childhood, about a bat's proclivity for flying into your hair and becoming frantically entangled. According to the article, however, bats are shy, and are, in fact, among the gentlest of creatures, "almost as soft as chincilla" to the touch. Some live to be thirty years old, putting them among the longest-lived mammals on earth. A mother bat usually rears only one pup a year and the male and female take turns with child rearing. The reporter wrote:

> Since they don't build nests, they take shelter in a wide range of secluded places. . . . When the females are giving birth and raising their young, they prefer warm places. . . . And since most bats produce only one baby a year, it's very important whether that baby survives or not.

Mon Dieu! What had we done to the poor *chauves-souris*? I was overcome with remorse, and sent the article to Jean, the home wrecker. (I made no mention of the brothel in my letter.)

In time, the bats—who had picked up stakes and never returned—were followed by other creatures.

Getting
Acquainted

4

MARKETING

Cooking may not be everyone's ideal way to spend a vacation, but it is mine. A gourmand's passion originates either from being brought up by a good cook or from deprivation. In my case, it was the latter. Not that my family was poor—far from it. I grew up in an upper-middle-class Midwestern suburb. But my mother had cooked her way through my two older brothers' lives and, during my childhood, had had to adjust to the restricted diet my father required after a serious heart attack. On holidays—dreaded holidays, in an atmosphere fraught with family friction—she would put on the requisite festive show, but our normal fare was, say, broiled chicken, a Bird's Eye frozen vegetable, and a salad, often eaten in the stony silence imposed by my father's mood. Friday-night specials, adhering to the Catholic Church's strictures, were frozen fish sticks—or a dish I remember with some fondness but would never cook—a casserole of canned tuna mixed with cream-of-mushroom soup and topped with crushed cornflakes.

This was a time when my idea of heaven was what in the Midwest was called a brown cow, a tall glass of foamy root beer with a scoop of vanilla ice cream. I had this every night before bed in summertime, sitting at the Formica-top table in the kitchen near the open window to the backyard, slurping to the tune of katydids and hypnotized by the blinking of lightning bugs (whose sticky golden corrugated "lights" Christine and I would amputate and try to wear as rings). *Katydid, katydidn't,* the insects chanted naughtily. And I would long for my grandmother Kate (my mother's mother and my only surviving grandparent), who lived in the rambling old house in Jerseyville, Illinois, where my mother was born. She always had a batch of warm cookies waiting for me in the pantry, where I could look out the window onto a vista of endless cornfields. When I visited her, I was content to do nothing but sit in a prickly green upholstered chair in the living room, shaking a glass paperweight to make snow fall on the tiny figures of a bride and groom. It was just us three in that house: my mother, my grandmother, and me, and there I was safe.

When I moved to New York two years after college, its culinary riches overwhelmed me. I'd never even heard of lox and bagels. My first deli lunch consisted of chopped chicken liver on rye. It looked dry, so I asked the counterman for ketchup. He looked as if I'd broken his heart. Missouri, Mars. On my first blind date—with a preppy Wall Street type—I ordered my first stuffed artichoke at the intimate Upper East Side French restaurant where he'd taken me to dinner. Logic said to eat it leaf by leaf, that is, *entire* leaf by entire leaf. I stopped when one caught in my windpipe. You learn.

Thereafter, I plunged into my food education unreservedly, even taking cooking courses during vacations: in France (at Le Cordon Bleu, during a two-month leave of absence from my job), Italy, and Mexico.

Now, with the luxury of a house in France, food has become paramount. No sooner have I finished breakfast than I'm thinking of the possibilities for lunch. Lunch hardly digested, I'm pondering dinner. Breakfast usually consists of toast made from a robust *pain de campagne*, with country butter and the fig or prune jam that is a specialty of the region. And coffee, of course. On some mornings I take a little ten-minute spin by car to the Counoud bakery in Bétaille, a village near Carennac, for one of its meltingly tender *pains aux raisins*, fresh out of the oven. Madame Counoud, a fresh-faced young woman, is always ready with a cheery greeting (I have spied her husband in his baker's outfit, and a young boy, in the back room). She picks up the roll, and with that deft gesture every bakery attendant has mastered, spins it in a fragile square of tissue, leaving two little twisted tufts to lock it in. On the way home, the tissue picks up smudges of butteriness and the car is filled with the mouthwatering scents of yeast, butter, and sweet warm raisins.

Occasionally, I'll even drive to St-Céré, a twenty-minute trip, for a croissant. One of the bakeries doubles as a little *salon de thé*, with a few tables and chairs in the rear. The young baker and his wife, along with their small son, live in the back. They serve a wonderful *café au lait*—the hiss of the coffee machine, which steams the milk, assures a *vrai café au lait*. Saturday and Sunday mornings are reserved for a late, big breakfast at the house, with toast and farm eggs. The eggs are remarkable, with golden-orange yolks, in contrast to the pale yellow of American store-bought eggs. The shells are so sturdy that once, when I had some left over at the end of a trip, I carried them back in my knapsack on the plane. The eggs are best in their purest form: soft-boiled.

On weekdays I make a steady round of the various *jours du marché* (in the cabinet, along with "Points on the Obvious and Obscure," is a list of village market days, covering an approximately sixty-kilometer radius). These vary in size, some consisting of only a half-dozen farmers gathered in the village square, offering fruits and vegetables, others including those with chickens and rabbits (some live, some dressed). St-Céré has a sizable market on the second Wednesday of each month, which features not only clothes and cutlery but a cattle sale. Once, I approached the roped-off area near the bridge over the river, curious about how much a cow might cost. Soon enough, I realized that this was a world that a single female, not to mention an American, could never penetrate. Rugged, weathered-looking farmers, with muddied boots and clothes, sun-bronzed faces, and dirt-encrusted, thick yellow fingernails, bargained and bartered—and, it appeared, chewed the fat—among themselves. They wrestled with the recalcitrant animals to examine them (lifting tails to assess hindquarters, prying open jaws), and slapped and tugged at the witless creatures as they led them away. Some of the beasts had blinders of old burlap sacks. This was a rough business; I drifted off.

The nonpareil market is held on Saturdays in Brive. I'm on the road by eight A.M., to be there in time for the best selection (village markets shut down by noon). By nine A.M., Brive—whose old town is situated like the hub of a wheel—is a beehive of activity. On the northern fringe of town, the market starts at a lot about the size of a football field, with stall after stall covered with canvas awnings in case of inclement weather, offering clothing and kitchen supplies. I move swiftly past shoppers for these goods to what makes my heart beat faster—the food. A group of trucks and stands leads to the indoor market, a great hall with long tables laden with produce—not only fresh fruits and vegetables, but bottled and tinned regional products reminding you that this is goose and duck country. This in turn spills out into another vast outdoor area in the rear, where, in addition to a field of more food stands, are purveyors of live birds and rabbits, flowers and plants. It is the most colorful, lively part of the market, so I usually do most of my shopping there.

The farmers are a friendly, cheery lot, patient and chatty with customers, yet swift when tallying prices. Weighing is done in time-honored fashion, on metal scales, which look so wobbly and wiggly that I'm baffled by their precision. The farmer holds the scale—a bar with two saucers attached by chains on each side—with one arm. He then balances the produce placed in one metal plate with metal weights in the opposite plate—this accomplished without a third arm. The whole operation strikes me as fussy and awkward.

I am often the butt of gentle—and sometimes not-so-gentle—teasing, since being single, I purchase relatively insignificant amounts. I often buy more than I need in order to meet a minimum. Sometimes I'm not charged for a few potatoes, a small bunch of parsley.

I first focus my efforts on the main course of what has become my traditional Saturday dinner: roast chicken. Chickens are not an inexpensive item. There are any number of rather upscale farmers who advertise an advanced feed formula for their chickens, but I seek out one of the elderly women (already scarce, and increasingly rare), weathered and garbed in black, who have brought their few chickens to market and posted a little handwritten cardboard sign, NOURRITURE EN GRAIN, on their table. Their birds are yellow and thick-skinned, not quite as plump and pale as the others. These are the most extraordinary chickens I've ever tasted, moist and flavorful (I imagine them pecking on fallen apples and crushed walnuts along with corn). This bird has become the *specialité chez moi*—Jean had been treated to it—stuffed with a whole head of aromatic lavender garlic, slices of lemon, and sprigs of pungent fresh rosemary that perfume my fingers for hours. Basted with country butter and olive oil, its thick skin becomes golden and crackling. The *queue* in France is reserved for the guest of honor— usually me. It is gelatinous, chewy, fatty—in other words, as delicious as it is sinfully cholesterol-laden.

Having secured the main course, I then concentrate on the pick of seasonal vegetables. In the spring, there are mounds after mounds of fat white asparagus; rows of lettuce in various hues of green, some fringed with red; early tomatoes from the Midi. The fall features *cèpes*, wonderful meaty mushrooms; cream-and-lavender turnips; pencil-thin green beans called *haricots verts*. At that time of year the hands of the farm women are stained mahogany from gathering walnuts, a specialty of the region that goes into oil, cakes and candies, and liqueurs. There are always varieties of potatoes, but best are the tiny, thumb-size ones which, sautéed, become creamy within their wilted skins.

Eggs often still have a bit of barnyard muck and even

an occasional feather adhering to the shell. Once, one of the farmers, in an act of great generosity, parted with a plastic container for a half-dozen eggs; this is a treasure (cartons are never provided with the sale of eggs) and I save it for carrying to market each time I go. Unpasteurized milk, measured out from big stainless-steel buckets, makes the creamiest scrambled eggs. Thick *crème fraîche*, which is unpourable heavy cream, cries out for strawberries. Many of the farmers offer their own *rillettes*, which are scraps of preserved duck or goose meat packed in the natural fat—delicious on hot toast that dissolves the fat (a sometime item on the hearty-breakfast menu). Small pots or tins of this are arranged beside fresh duck breasts. I sauté duck breasts in the skillet and finish them with a sauce of orange juice and port wine. Then the fruits: grapefruit and oranges, and in the spring wonderful blood oranges, and apples and pears, which make a good marriage with *cabecou*. The ubiquitous goat cheese of the region, *cabecou* is offered in various stages of aging: the youngest bitter, the oldest crustier and saltier. I prefer *cabecou crémeau*, which is midway between the two.

Normally, I depend on a neighbor for *cabecou*. One spring morning, not long after I'd bought the house, I was running my usual route in the valley to the village of Puybrun, where the *notaire* lives. At one juncture, where the road goes practically by the doorstep of a farmhouse and barn, a distinct lactic smell struck my nostrils. I came to a dead halt. Cheese. Then I spotted black-and-white goats grazing in a field by the house. *Cabecou.* I sprinted up the steps and rang the bell. A young woman, wiping her hands on her apron, opened the door and gave me a look of surprise. My outfit—a T-shirt and jogging shorts—is somewhat startling attire in these parts.

I explained that I was American and owned the little house on the hill. Her road, I said with a flattening gesture, was a good one for jogging. She nodded with a hesitant smile. I got to the point. Had I smelled cheese?

She laughed, patting her palms on her stomach as if that's where the cheese resided. Yes, she said, I had smelled *cabecou*. The cheese, however, was not sold here, but rather at a relative's house. She gave me directions to the place.

I showered and changed before I drove back to the valley. The rather drab two-story house was located at the end of a pitted, muddy drive. As I stepped from the car a wiry gray-and-white dog came tearing around the side of the house, skidding to an abrupt halt at my heels, barking madly. He sprang back and forth, like a windup toy, snapping at the air around me, his bark growing hoarse. *"Bon chien,"* I said, in the gentlest, most lyrical tone I could muster. *"Bon chien. Bon chien."* This only enraged him more. I stood my ground, motionless except for my rapid breathing. Minutes passed. Finally, from the house across the way, a woman emerged and toddled along a roundabout walkway.

"Jules, Jules, shoosh, shoosh," she called out sweetly as she approached.

I offered a staccato explanation above the still-shrilling beast: American, house on the hill, the run, the request for *cabecou*.

She smiled broadly. *"Allez,"* she said, motioning me to follow her in the direction of a small shack. Jules was still leaping and yapping furiously. I didn't budge.

"Il n'est pas méchant?" I called out to her retreating back.

"Jules, Jules, assez." She waved me forward. I took a

tentative step and the dog desisted, following his mistress begrudgingly, with a backward look at me as if to say, "*You*, watch your p's and q's."

She opened the door to the shack, leaving Jules to stand guard outside. It was as cool and fresh as the inside of a refrigerator. The aroma was yeasty and pungent. She asked at what stage of aging I preferred my *cabecou*. Then she went to a small back room and returned with a tray of the tiny disks of cheese, which, by regulation, have to be about two inches in diameter and about a half inch thick. These had a pristine look about them—like solidified milk with a tender skin—unlike the slightly firmer version I'd bought at market. I asked for four. She wrapped them carefully in white paper and escorted me to the car, past a sulking Jules.

It was nearly noon. I decided that for lunch with my *cabecou*, I would buy a crusty loaf of bread and some ripe tomatoes. I poured a glass of red wine, toasted the bread, and placed a slab of *cabecou* on top. I pressed it gently with a knife to spread it a bit. It oozed, a smooth, creamy river, to the edge of the toast. I quickly took a bite. I had had fine *cabecou* many, many times. But this was unlike any I'd ever tasted: a little tart because of the freshness of the goat's milk, slightly piquant from the grasses on which the goats fed. I was addicted. Thereafter, going for *cabecou* was one of my first errands upon arriving at the house.

Jules, however, never accepted me as a regular and I never warmed to him either. He put on the same show each time. And each time I waited for his mistress to give me the go-ahead.

Since the Brive market offers seasonal produce, there is seemingly endless repetition among the sellers. Yet I always cover the territory before making purchases, often discovering variables: a different variety of pear, a fatter bunch of asparagus. And from time to time surprises pop up, such as, once, a single basket of exotically speckled quail eggs. One year there was a delicious raisin *confiture*, but the farm woman who made it never reappeared. One late November I encountered a truffle man, who sold me a walnut-sized piece at a bargain price. I sliced it as thin as possible (lacking a truffle shaver) and slipped it under the skin of my chicken before roasting, emulating a mode of preparation called *en demi-deuil* (in half mourning). What must be the most earthy version of *demi-deuil* was a specialty of Fernand Point (1897–1955), whose Pyramide restaurant, in Vienne, was considered a bastion of twentieth-century French cuisine. His *poulet de Bresse truffé en vessie* became one of his signature dishes and is still on the menu today. The entire chicken is larded with truffles and baked inside a cow's bladder. In my humble kitchen I could honor a hallowed tradition. That night I opened a special bottle of white Burgundy.

Finally, I can never resist a bouquet of flowers, which I'm reduced to locking under an armpit, my shopping basket by then overflowing. The trip back to the car is a lame-gaited walk.

By car, I would make a final stop at Monsieur Barrique's, the best wine merchant in town until his recent demise, and one of the *pâtissiers* (each with a *specialité de la maison*) for dessert, my favorite being miniature tarts made from freshly ground walnuts. Then I'm on my way, with a big appetite. On the drive back, I do a mental to-do list: store things in the refrigerator, grind the coffee beans, light the oven (I want warm bread), squeeze the oranges, dust the chicken livers with flour. . . .

The size of my kitchen approximates that of a New York studio apartment, which is to say, suitable for one person with just enough room to turn around in. It has, as I've said, a half refrigerator, a small counter with overhead cabinets, a tiny sink with shelves beneath, and a two-burner oven. There is a bitty window over the oven for ventilation and an average-size window overlooking the side yard; I gaze directly outdoors when I wash the dishes. In the spring, with the window wide-open, insects of every stripe light on the ledge or counter; as long as they don't interfere, I let them be. Except spiders, which I gently herd out the window with a paper towel. When a daddy longlegs appears, with its pinhead body and absurdly ill-proportioned high arched legs, it's as if I'm visited by a miniature carnival carousel. How can these creatures go through life on such fragile supports? Once, I turned on the faucet, unaware that one was crouched in the sink. It wilted to a heartbreaking bundle of legs.

Kitchen here is galley. The advantage is that everything is within arm's reach. And I can state unabashedly that some of the best meals of my life came out of that pint-size room.

As well as, once, a disaster, when I had a bout of food poisoning after eating an over-the-hill sausage called *merguez*. It was then that I learned, however, that one does not get sick from French food. When I reported my problem (*intoxication alimentaire*; I had looked it up) to the pharmacist, he nodded appreciatively and said, "Ah, oui, la crise de foie."

The French are known for their fixation on the liver; *la crise de foie* is as familiar as our common cold. A lesson in one of my French exercise books depicts a scene similar to mine in the pharmacy. Only there is no mention of food poisoning. Food poisoning? Despite the fact that it's in the dictionary, it does not exist in France.

The multitude of village food festivals is testimony to the average Frenchman's culinary appreciation. A couple of years ago, for example, there was a *fête de la noix*, held on a Sunday afternoon in October. It took place in nearby Saillac, a small circle of a village with an especially charming little church. The festival promised—I came upon flyers in a local shop—an *omelette géante*. When I arrived, I discovered that *tout le monde* was there—the only spot for the car was down a country lane some distance away.

On this sunny, warm day, the single restaurant was bursting at its seams, with midday diners spilling onto tables set up outdoors. Under a little tent in the center of the village, merchants were also selling anything and everything made from walnuts: *pâtés*, cookies, cakes, oils, liqueurs, and so on. A complete sucker for festival takeouts, I typically load up with more than I can possibly consume. As a child of parents who had lived through the Depression, perhaps I caught something of their stocking-up instincts. Or something of my father's fetish for mail-order goods, a habit that far outpaced our small family's consumption.

The preparation of the *omelette géante* was announced for four o'clock. It was to take place on a stretch of roadway on the far side of a stone wall by the tent. As the hour approached, the crowds began migrating in that direction, jockeying for prized positions on top of the stone wall.

The *omelette géante*, I learned, would consist of four

thousand eggs. I couldn't get my mind around this numbing figure. What would four thousand eggs look like? How were they amassed? Had every chicken house in the Lot been cleaned out?

In the center of the road was a narrow waist-high metal trough, perhaps sixty feet long, affixed with gas jets. Perhaps a dozen men and women involved in the preparation were gathered alongside. At the appointed hour they began unloading cardboard cartons of eggs, each containing three hundred and fifty eggs. It was a hailstorm of eggs. Standing over or seated by enormous plastic buckets and pails—some the size of New York City garbage cans—they began cracking the eggs. One gentleman, who was particularly dexterous, could crack two eggs in each hand at the same time. The scene of people and eggs was something out of a fairy tale or, even more bizarrely, out of a Bosch painting. This went on for nearly an hour. As the buckets filled up, members of the crew began beating them with giant hand whisks or electric beaters. Finally, bushels of chopped walnuts—which were, after all, the point of the festival—were stirred in. The gas jets were lit. As the trough heated up, oil was poured in. When the agreed-upon moment for cooking the omelette arrived, a small brass band, smartly decked out in white uniforms with gold-braided caps, struck up a rousing oompah-pah. This had the effect of a start button: kids began scampering about, dogs started yapping, cameras began flashing. The *omelette géante* went on the fire. A half-dozen men, stationed alongside the trough, stirred it with great paddles—like cooking with shovels— over gas jets that had to be constantly adjusted.

There was plenty to go around. It was delicious: creamy, with the slight crunch of walnuts. Plus, an omelette eaten while leaning against an old stone wall in the sunshine is never bad.

When I reported on the festival to the Hirondes, they were duly impressed, and seemed a little disappointed to have missed it. They'd spent the afternoon at a strawberry festival and had found the *tartes aux fraises* substandard.

5

THE STAFF OF LIFE

My part of France, the Lot, is superb bread country. Privately, I conduct an ongoing Best Bread Contest. For a while the Bétaille bakery headed the list. Its *pain de campagne* is a slightly domed loaf with a crisp crust that shatters when you slice into it and a dense interior. Then I advanced a bakery in St-Céré into first place, when, one noon, I picked up half of a fat saucer of warm *pain de campagne*. It had a moist yeastiness that Bétaille's lacked.

Though it was somewhat beyond the realm of my survey, on a trip to the neighboring *département* of the Dordogne in the early spring of 1987, I went out of my way to visit the village of Meyrals, having read some travel piece claiming its bakery had "the best bread in the region." I was the first through the door when the tiny *boulangerie* opened—a cold, gray, foggy morning that called out for a comforting *café au lait*. I chose a *pain de campagne* the size of an automobile tire's hub, stashed it in the backseat, and set off for Pech Farguet. On the way back, reason set in—I'd bought more than I could possibly eat before it went stale.

I stopped at the Hirondes. After reviewing my trip to the Dordogne, I mentioned my purchase of what I'd heard was a superior bread. Would they care to try some?

They looked at me rather blankly and politely declined.

I asked which bread they regarded as The Best.

Bétaille's, they agreed without hesitation.

I then explained that I'd probably bought too much of the Dordogne bread. Did they by chance have a freezer, where I might store a portion? Then I could take it back to the States when I left at the end of the week.

They stared at me, barely masking their incredulity. The notion of freezing bread—in a country where you went daily for your noon and evening *baguette*—was apparently a novel one. They didn't have a freezer, but the Servais did.

The Servais had no real interest in sampling another *département*'s bread either. I interviewed them on their opinion of The Best Bread.

They paused gravely before answering. St-Céré's *boulangerie* near the Coq Arlequin restaurant had probably the best, in their opinion. Yes, no question about it.

Madame agreed cheerily to freeze my bread.

"YOO 'AVE NO BREAD IN YUR COUNTREE?" Monsieur asked.

A few years ago, at one of the Wednesday markets in St-Céré, I sampled an enormous (of basketball dimensions) loaf I purchased from one of the traveling salesmen and had to further refine my list. It was the tops, with a rugged crust and a nutty, moist interior with big holes, as if the dough had belched and stretched in the oven.

The young man grinned proudly when I said it was the best bread I'd tasted. Was there a way to purchase it on a more regular basis? I asked. He replied that his father made the bread and that his bakery, with its wood-burning oven, was located near Martel. On Fridays, I could purchase it there. The name was Rauley.

"*Près de Martel!*" I exploded joyfully. Martel was a mere half-hour drive from my house.

"*À Cabriole, près de Quatres Routes,*" he said more precisely, and wrote the name on a slip of paper.

I was leaving before the following Friday, so I had to put off the excursion until the following fall. Then—a penetratingly cold Friday morning when the mist in the valley refused to budge—I studied my map and set out for Rauley's bakery. I relish a mission; I love a find. At Quatres Routes, I passed a sign for Cabriole and took the winding road uphill. This took me past a small cluster of houses and farms. There was no bakery in sight—nothing of a commercial nature. It seemed that Cabriole was not a village but a little hamlet. I circled back. Not a soul was outdoors, so I started back to Quatres Routes to inquire. Along the way I spotted some men repairing the road.

I tooted my horn. "*Je cherche la boulangerie à Cabriole,*" I shouted to the group, hanging my head out the rolled-down window. The toot, and my accented French, momentarily stunned them. Then one of the men came forward.

"*La boulangerie?*" he said, doffing his cap.

"*Oui, Monsieur Rauley, pour son pain,*" I said, hopes dimmed but undashed.

"*Eh, beang, Rauley! Le garage, à droit.*"

Garage? Why garage? Could this be right?

"Le pain, c'est bon!" He waved. This was encouraging, but confusing. I circled back in the direction he'd pointed, which was simply retracing my route. Once again in Cabriole, I saw on the right what could be taken for a garage—a graveyard of run-down, antiquated cars. I turned in. There was a ramshackle farmhouse and a small barn. Chickens and ducks scurried crazily in the car's path. A peacock was perched incongruously on a retired tractor. When I slammed the car door, it fanned its glorious tail.

The crisp autumn air carried aromas of baking bread. Could this be the place after all? I followed the scent to a small barn—the *boulangerie?* Rapping on the door, I waited, but there was no response. I could hear movement from within, so I tried the latch. A giant of a man stood with his back to me, shoveling bread with a long paddle from the open oven and stacking the loaves on open wooden shelves. Due to a severely shortened leg, he careened as he moved back and forth, his body skewed like the Hunchback of Notre Dame. He was oblivious to my presence.

"Monsieur?" I said hesitantly, but he didn't respond. Apparently he was hard of hearing. How could I approach him without startling him? I made a wide circle and came up alongside his stooped figure by the oven.

"Monsieur Rauley?" I repeated in a loud voice.

He righted himself and stared fixedly at the apparition that had invaded his premises.

"Je viens acheter votre pain," I explained, pointing emphatically to the bread. *"Le meilleur pain du monde."* I smiled winningly, hoping to get us past the awkward moment.

With the barest flicker of an expression, he opened the

oven door, to show me the grand glowing-brick interior. The smell was as good as smells get, like new-mown grass, the air before rain.

"*Grand ou petit!*" he boomed.

"*Petit,*" I replied (*petit* being about the size of a large dinner plate).

"*Froid ou chaud?*" he then asked.

This threw me for a minute. Warm was inherently more appealing, but what would be the point, since it would cool off on the drive home?

"*Froid,*" I said.

He chose a loaf from the shelf and weighed it on a small scale. In paying, I accidentally handed him a quarter instead of a franc. Seeing my mistake, I quickly explained the error.

"*C'est le même?*" he asked.

"*À peu près,*" I said, with a wavy motion of the hand.

He preferred the American quarter. He polished it on the sleeve of his jacket as he opened the door for me.

Rauley's bread took the blue ribbon that year, *vaut le voyage* (worth the trip), in Michelin terms. It was immensely satisfying to know it was never far away.

The quest, nonetheless, is never ending. As I approached the covered market in Brive on a sunny morning the following May, I passed a dairy truck whose owner was gazing off into space with a look of contentment on his face, evidently savoring his *petit déjeuner:* a hefty *tranche* of bread and slices of *saucisson* impaled on the point of a sharp knife, which he deskewered with his teeth. I reached up—a gesture that summons up a childhood sensation of diminutiveness, paying for candy in the drugstore—to place the change for a purchase of *comté* cheese in his outstretched palm. I asked who he thought had the best bread in the market.

He pointed to a small truck across the way.

"*Le meilleur,*" he pronounced unhesitatingly. "*Même dans leur forme bizarre,*" he added.

Most bread sellers in the market offer other items, such as cakes and rolls, laid out on long wooden tables. This purveyor sold nothing but bread, which I took as a positive sign of singular devotion. In the open trunk of the small van were stacks of bread, but the line was long and they were going fast. Monsieur was right. I had never seen bread in such a variety of shapes, as if the dough had been tossed and slapped around—clearly the work of the hand—and shoveled into the oven in whatever shape it landed. They had the look of old leather shoes, misshapen and craggy, with shiny, smooth "soles" in an ashen-gray color.

When my turn came, I quickly asked the robust woman in a blue smock if all the bread was the same. Did I hear titters from the line?

"*Ben, oui.*" She nodded. "*Épais ou mince?*" A choice of thick or thin—a question, really, of more dough or more crust. It was a heated moment, with the press of the waiting customers at my heels. "*Mince,*" the woman behind me prodded.

"*Épais,*" I found myself saying. "*Mais plus petit?*" I pleaded as she picked up a loaf the size of a garbage-pail lid.

"*La moitié?*" she asked, knife poised.

At the first bite, I judged it the best bread on the face of the earth. It combined all the qualities of the other great *pains de campagne:* moist, yeasty, wheaty, with a pocked interior and rugged crust. The "sole" of this bread gave it extra character and chewiness.

When the next Saturday rolled around, I headed for Brive. My last stop was the bread truck. And there, big as life, was Monsieur Rauley serving the steady line of customers. I waited my turn.

"*C'est vous!*" I exclaimed.

He looked nonplussed.

I reminded him of my visit to his place.

"*Peut-être.*" He shrugged—as if to say, maybe I had been there, maybe not.

Little did Rauley realize that he had beat himself in the Best Bread Contest. That's when I more or less abandoned the whole idea of a competition—where had painstaking objectivity got me? The real winner, I decided, was the *département* of the Lot, where the great bread of France is found. Despite France's reputation as a shrine to superb bread, I've tasted plenty of thin-crusted, cottony examples in other regions, even the neighboring Dordogne, also notable for its gastronomic riches. I'd even go so far as to say that Poilane, the renowned baker in Paris, can't match Rauley's. Just one former judge's opinion.

6

HOUSE
IMPROVEMENTS

O wning a house, *c'est toujours quelque chose*, as they say. Often, I feel, my days are spent running from plumber, to bank, to carpenter, to bank, to the *épicerie* because I'm out of coffee, and so on. Trips are a combination of household business—from which I nonetheless derive a certain satisfaction since it is performed on foreign turf—and pleasure. I do read—or at least I sit with a book from time to time. Yet my degree of concentration is different in France. When I read on the subway to and from work in New York, I can burrow into a book and block out the world around me, including the crackling incomprehensible public addresses and vociferous panhandlers and preachers. At Pech Farguet, if I sit on the patio, my eyes will drift from the page to the view of the valley, or my ears will perk up at an unusual birdsong; if I sit in the chair by the fireplace, my thoughts wander to the next meal or are interrupted by the mysterious patter of feet on the roof. My eyes have traveled the words but not read.

There is one book, however, that held me rapt for a long spell: *Animal Treasure*, by Ivan T. Sanderson, published in 1937, with thirty-two illustrations by its British author. I stumbled on it—the cover slightly warped and the pages a parchmentlike color—in an antiques shop in Bretenoux. Inside, its former owner had written, *This book belongs to H. P. Mussell*. From its opening sentence I was hooked: "The animals that crowd their little faces into the following pages lived, or are still living, in the deep virgin forests of West Africa, around a place called Mamfe, a place known to but a handful of the earth's inhabitants." The author then clearly states his viewpoint: to study both the true geneological classification of animals and the natural (or ecological) classifications. While this may seem to be purely scientific interest, it is, in fact, a highly personal account, by turns witty and poignant, of the author's adventures with both beasts and fellow explorers.

Here is a passage—Sanderson's reaction to a dead gorilla—that has to be among the most moving in all of such literature:

I had always been taught to think of the gorilla as the very essence of savagery and terror, and now there lay this hoary old vegetarian, his immense arms folded over his great pot belly, all the fire gone from his wrinkled black face, his soft brown eyes wide open beneath their long straight lashes and filled with an infinite sorrow. Into his whole demeanor I could not help but read the tragedy of his race, driven from the plains up into the mountains countless centuries ago by more ac-

tive ape-like creatures—perhaps even our own fore-
bears; chevied hither and thither by the ever-
encroaching hordes of hairless shouting little men, his
young ones snatched by leopards, his feeding grounds
restricted by farms and paths and native huntsmen. All
around him was a changing world against which he
bellowed his defiance to the end, rushing forward to
eject the bits of lead and gravel blasted at him by his
puny rival.

At last the Munchis came and the sad old man was
lashed to two young trees and borne away by thirty
staggering, chanting humans; away from the silence of
the mists, away from his last tangled stronghold; and
yet not quite the last of the giants and not quite
unmourned.

I would often put the book down to absorb what I'd
just read. It was *too* good; I wanted it to stick with me.
I savored the book over two years (I leave it at the
house), tasting it in small doses.

Generally, I read at the end of the day, around sundown,
when I'm winding down, or at bedtime when it will put
me to sleep. Otherwise, there is always something that
takes up a day. A day can seem short, a day can seem
endless. When I return to New York, I feel I've been gone
a long time, which, I think, has to do with the way I
spend my vacation, living an everyday existence in another country rather than bustling about sightseeing.

In May of 1988, there was added "business" to attend
to. I had invited my cousin Marilyn (Munsterman, on my
mother's side) and her husband, Charles Berberich, to
visit the house. They live in Denver and are real Franco-

philes, Charles especially, who speaks fluent French and whose aunt and uncle lived in France for years. I wanted the house to look its best. I washed the windows, brought curtains and bedspread to the *blanchisserie*, replaced a missing coffee cup. Then I decided to purchase some heavy-duty oilcloth to cover two wine racks in the *cave*.

I drove into the kitchen-and-household-supply store in St-Céré, an expansive two-story affair carrying everything from hibachis to double boilers. I approached the female cashier on the first level. I had unfortunately neglected to arm myself with the word for oilcloth, which was not part of my standard vocabulary. I suspected that *huile*, the word for oil, would be vastly misleading, so I put together a broad description of what I was seeking: thick, shiny, plastic-coated paper. Something like that. She understood instantly. That would be on the second floor. There I approached the service counter and repeated my request to Madame. She, too, understood immediately what I was after. She pointed to the rear of the floor. *"Choisissez votre dessin,"* she instructed me cheerily. At the rear of the shop, sure enough, there was an entire rack of more than a dozen oilcloths, one above the other, each slightly unrolled to display the various patterns. I mulled over the selection and eventually settled on one that I felt would show the least soiling. I returned to the service desk.

"J'ai choisi le dessin," I announced.

"Bon," she said. *"Portez-le ici, s'il vous plaît."*

This was rather puzzling, but I took her at her word—to bring the roll—and returned to the rack. The rolls, perhaps four feet long, were anchored one on top of the other with steel rods that were attached to heavy metal hooks at each end. I grasped the one I'd chosen and hoisted it off the rack, releasing it from the mean-looking hooks. It was tremendously heavy. I had to let one end drop to the floor and dragged the fat monster, the metal rod whining, under my arm toward the service counter. As I approached it, stooped and limping with my burden, I sensed a sudden stillness in the room. A pair of customers in one aisle, a small group around the service desk, and Madame herself were all standing motionless, their eyes trained on me. They looked as if they were holding still for me to take a photograph of them. Something was terribly wrong. Madame rushed to assist me for the final lap.

"*Oh, madame,*" she said, oddly mournful. Then she explained. She thought I'd wanted *shelving* paper. A thousand apologies. Of course, I'd used the word *papier*, which had misled everyone.

Mortification. And then, deepening my humiliation, she said, with a well of pity, "*Pauvre madame.*" It was one of those moments when you come smack up against your foreignness. When I got home, I looked up the word for oilcloth: *toile cirée*. It is now firmly fixed in memory.

After that, I focused on the floor in the main room. It had been stained a deep mahogany (the old-world English look) and was sorely scuffed. What an improvement it would be to have it stripped and varnished in a soft, lighter finish (the Early American natural look). It would brighten and freshen up the whole room.

To accomplish this job required a further extension of my vocabulary. I prepared myself this time with a new batch of words: *enlever* (strip off), *vernis* (varnish), and the like. At the paint store in St-Céré, the woman directed me to a lumberyard on the edge of town.

"Bien sûr." Monsieur nodded when I arrived and had stated my needs. *"Vous voudrez poncer le plancher."* *Poncer le plancher.* The words bounced in my head—it sounded like a circus act. He proposed to send a man to the house to give me an estimate. The best way to give directions to my house, I have learned, is to draw a little map: the bridge over the Dordogne, the right turn to Carennac, a left at the fork, the stone wall at the very top of the winding road, the dirt road and the first crossroad, the left turn and the *very* steep descent to the house. To emphasize the steepness, I always crook an arm at a sixty-degree angle. The appointment with a Monsieur Barrié was set for the following morning.

After breakfast, I sat on the patio awaiting his arrival. Soon I heard a car at the intersection and the crunch of gravel as it descended. Monsieur Barrié stepped out of his car with a young man whom he introduced as his son. Monsieur had curly reddish hair and a pale complexion, unusual coloring for this part of France. This was echoed in his son, a painfully thin young man who languidly chain-smoked.

Inside the house, Monsieur admired, pro forma, the view from the windows, and then proceeded to take measurements. He walked mincingly, heel to toe, heel to toe—as the average person would in trying to get a rough estimate of feet—the length and breadth of the room. This struck me as a rather casual method—especially since I would be charged according to this measurement. With a flourish, he made calculations on a notepad and presented me with a figure. The entire job required stripping the floor of the old varnish, applying two new coats, and polishing; this would take two days. I had not expected to spend that much money, but by now my excitement about the project overcame any second thoughts.

Also, this would fit in perfectly with a plan I'd made for a brief canoeing expedition on the Dordogne. (I make it a rule to steal away for at least two or three days of *real* vacation on each trip.) The job could all be accomplished, painlessly, while I was away.

Monsieur said he would prepare a bill and arrive the next day at nine A.M. We said our farewells.

The road going past my house down to the valley, as I always emphasize in directions, is treacherously steep; in a shift car, you need to remain in first gear. I forewarn anyone who's not been there. Upon their departure, I advise them—as I now did Monsieur Barrié—to continue downhill, past the Salgues' farm, and circle back to the main road, rather than attempt the impossible uphill return. But no sooner had I closed the door than I heard the squeal of spinning wheels and the sputter of flying gravel. For some reason—sheer obstinateness? a streak of machismo?—he had reversed the car and attempted to head up the hill. I rushed out to the alarming sight of Monsieur Barrié's car tilted crazily at the side of the road. It had skidded backward and now teetered at the edge of a drop-off to the valley below. He was standing by the car, with a ghostly pallor, wiping his brow with a handkerchief. His son remained seated in the passenger seat, his head propped against the headrest, smoking unconcernedly.

"Attendez!" I shouted. *"Je vais chez Monsieur Hironde!"* Hironde, I reasoned, who had so capably delivered wood to my house, going down *and* back up the road with his tractor, could surely help.

I walked/ran to the Hirondes' and found Raymond in his yard. Hyperventilating, I attempted to explain the situation: my left hand, the road, at an upward angle; my right hand, the car, sliding down, down, down. He responded with his usual aplomb and said he would arrive *tout de suite.*

Monsieur Barrié was staked out beside the car as if willing it to hold fast. At the arrival of Hironde and the tractor, he became visibly agitated, perhaps at the sight of the giant, rumbling vehicle, perhaps in response to Raymond's amazing calm. Hasty introductions made, Hironde pulled the tractor into the patch of lawn by the house, backed up, and turned the tractor in the uphill direction. (Tractors, of course, have no trouble with the ascent—I'd seen my neighbor Salgue negotiate it daily.) He then hitched a long, thick cable to the front fender of Barrié's car and instructed Barrié to return to the driver's seat. (The son, enveloped in a smoke cloud of disinterest, had never left the car.)

I retreated to the patio as the tractor began its sure, grumbling, turtlelike ascent. The car was plucked gently from the edge of the embankment. I slipped into the house and peeked out from behind the curtain, to save Monsieur Barrié my witnessing his humiliation. From the door, where the road is seen at its steepest, I watched as the tractor disappeared uphill behind the trees, with Barrié's car, cigarette smoke issuing from the window, inching along at the end of its tether.

Monsieur Barrié and his son arrived on schedule the following morning, with no mention of the previous day's escapade. I bade him farewell and set off for the canoeing expedition.

In New York, I had made arrangements for this short venture with the Safaraid company, who operate some six hundred boats in canoeing territory. After checking in at the seventeenth-century Château de la Treyne, in Pensac, where I had made reservations for the night, I stopped for an al fresco lunch at a totally deserted restaurant in Meyronne. I met my guide, Jean-Noël Dufour, a lithe young man with a shock of reddish hair and mustache, at his house in the nearby tiny village of St-Sozy. Right away he asked me to call him by his first name and proudly divulged that the house, which had been his family's second residence when they lived in Paris, was his inheritance. He preferred the country life.

Since there had been a surplus of rain in the spring, the river was high. Thus, rubber boots and a wet suit were essential. He pointed to a back room where I could slip into them. I wiggled in a sort of bizarre dance into the wet suit, a hideously viselike outfit; it was like being snapped up in a giant rubber band. I pulled on the boots, but then decided that they were on the wrong feet. I switched them and had the same sensation. I concluded that it didn't matter. Following Jean-Noël to the car, I rocked sideways with the gait of a robot, though he seemed oblivious to my condition, as agile in his own wet suit as if it were a second skin. He loaded the canoe on the rack of the car and we headed for the river. Sitting in the car in my rubber straitjacket, I felt like a crash-test dummy. A hot crash-test dummy. My skin couldn't breathe.

When we reached the river, Jean-Noël parked the car and maneuvered the canoe to the water as I waddled after him. At the shoreline he handed me a bright yellow life jacket, which transformed me into a buxom robot. Usually I enjoy the paraphernalia of a sport—the shoes and clothes for running, for example—but this was all so odious. I gracelessly boarded the rocking boat. Jean-Noël pushed off from shore, assuring me that the water would be *très tranquille*. I thirstily gulped the cool breezes as the canoe was picked up by the current. Jean-Noël captained from the rear, dexterously manipulating a double-paddle oar. My canoeing experience was limited to long-ago days in the Missouri Ozarks, where I had gone to summer camps as a kid. From the front of the boat, I dipped in my single-paddle oar from time to time, to one side or the other, feeling ineffectual. This actually suited me just fine. I was completely content acquainting myself with the river from this fish-eye view. The landscape of high bluffs and lush greenery slipped by. I felt I'd become a part of the scene in one of those timeless Missouri river paintings by George Caleb Bingham.

Only at one point did the river become less than *tranquille*. We ran into a sudden stretch of rapids and were swept pell-mell to shore. I sucked in my breath and clutched the sides of the canoe, in that split second grateful for the hideous wet suit. But Jean-Noël, unruffled, pushed us off again and we rejoined the quieter waters.

After an hour of gliding along, he steered into shore at the Île de la Borgne, a tiny deserted island with a carpet of wildflowers. He remarked that there are many such *sauvage* places in the country, but that there was nothing to fear. We hiked across the flat terrain for a view of Belcastel, a privately owned seventeenth-century château, perched like a hawk on the brink of a high overhanging cliff. Back on course, we continued on the tranquil four-mile trip to end up near Pensac and the château. More serious canoeists would have continued on to Souillac for a full-day trip, with a picnic along the way. But I had opted for this briefer excursion.

Jean-Noël dropped me off beneath a little bridge by the château (one of the help would later drive me to pick up my car). I struggled out of my life jacket, wet suit, and boots. Free at last. The air circulating about my body was deliciously refreshing. I felt as light as a butterfly. Thanking him, I waved good-bye and climbed up the steep bank to the bridge.

The view of the château was breathtaking. Though it seems precarious, on the very brink of a rocky precipice over the river, its solid base is actually strategically anchored. Its turrets and towers soar heavenward. I trudged up the hill and wandered about the garden before a light rain drove me inside. There I was effusively greeted by Madame Michèle Gombert-Devals, who owns and runs the château. Ah, she loved Carennac! She had friends there, whom I must meet. And how was my canoeing? I must tell her all about it. A pity, this dampening shower. Last November they'd been able to have dinner on the terrace. And why was my visit so brief? She so enjoyed company!

I wandered through the stately interior: billiards room, Renaissance salon, and library, all furnished with tapestries and ponderous antiques. One could easily imagine the rooms peopled with richly attired guests, who would have arrived by carriage and boat, attended by plumed servants in the candlelit interior. It was a romantic picture. But wouldn't travel have been tedious? How did they manage it, with all the trappings required then? Still, despite the ease with which I'd arrived, I was just as ready to be pampered.

Before dinner, I had an aperitif in the salon, where a fire burned steadily. The giant wheels of wood would burn for days. Contentment, after a full, unusual day. I took my place in the dining room, which overlooked a small formal garden. The room, which was decorated in the same grand manner as the rest, had a rather gloomy atmosphere, though Madame Gombert-Devals stopped solicitously at my table to wish me *bon appétit*.

It was one of the worst meals I've had in France. I had opted for the chef's menu of the day, which I expected to show him off at his best. Instead, it was sadly overambitious; he would have done well to let the food speak for itself. Why ruin *foie gras* with a salad drowning in vinaigrette? Why mask the flavor of the *gigot* of lamb with a blanket of rich sauce, crowded on the plate with a mushy *ratatouille*? A respectable Cantal, a nice Cahors wine, and a decent apple tart could not erase the overall sense of a missed opportunity. This was at first perplexing, since I regarded Madame Gombert-Devals as a woman of taste. On second thought, I realized that she was the sort of woman who wouldn't concern herself with *haute cuisine*. She was a people person. That was her focus, and her forte. (The chef was probably a dear friend whom she was encouraging in his delusions of, perhaps, the *septième*.)

The following day was Easter Sunday. I drove to Souillac for the eleven o'clock Mass at the cathedral. In the States, as I said, I never attend Mass, since I renounced Catholicism years ago. Yet, in France, I go both to partake in a ritual of French life and to sharpen my French by listening to the sermons.

The priest was standing with a plump altar boy to the right of the altar. Before the Mass began, a nun scurried up to the altar—slinking catlike, as if she wouldn't be noticed—to straighten the altar boy's cassock in an age-old motherly gesture. He blushed crimson. A group of musicians from Strasbourg were on hand for the holiday: the men on drums, horn, and trumpet, the women beautifully costumed with great ribbon hairpieces, black embroidered skirts, and lace-collared blouses. The music, however, was somewhat dispirited, and the women seemed to be there for decoration rather than to sing, as I'd anticipated.

Sermons are always a challenge. Without an immediate context to hang on to, I'm often at sea. This one, delivered theatrically, was based on an allegory involving astronauts that I never completely grasped. It had something to do with our being astronauts in a quest for the heavens (God), the need for training (religion), the stumbling blocks (temptations), and so on. Or, in the dark sea of the language, that's the message I came away with— greatly reduced, since the sermon went on for a good twenty minutes. During the Communion, accompanied by the repetitious music, I ducked out.

At Martel, nearing home, I stopped for lunch at La Turenne. *Tout le monde* was packed into the restaurant for a long holiday gourmandizing. I had a perfect grilled trout and a half bottle of Muscadet, watching the festivities. But I didn't dawdle. I was anxious to get home to see the floors.

The room was transformed! It was light, airy, cooler. I almost hated to walk on the floors, like eating just after you've had your teeth cleaned.

Then I noticed a little visitor, witness to my delight. A tiny blue-and-yellow bird was flitting about the kitchen, its head cocked in curiosity at my sudden presence. Fearlessly, it hopped to the window ledge and, with a little scolding twitter—why did you have to come home?—flew off.

Before preparing dinner, I stopped by the Hirondes in order to thank Monsieur for rescuing Monsieur Barrié. In thanks for my thanks, Simone gave me a jar of her luscious fat *cèpes*, which she had put up from the fall harvest. Seated at the dining-room table, Raymond jocularly reenacted the folly of the event—which called for an aperitif. At the end of the restaged drama, he shook his head. The man was a very bad driver, he pronounced. And *trop nerveux*.

The house looked splendid for Marilyn and Charles's arrival. They fell in love with Pech Farguet. They stayed at the Fénelon in Carennac for several nights at the tail end of my visit and the beginning of theirs. After I left, they moved to the house and stayed on for another couple of weeks of their vacation. It was "the sweetest corner in the world," Marilyn wrote on a postcard.

The following spring we planned our vacations to coincide for several days again, and after that they began to come in July for their summer holiday. They've grown to cherish Pech Farguet as much as I do. After one visit Marilyn wrote: "The stars, they tell a lot about the fun we had. The nights were so warm, and it stayed light so late. Perhaps we would drive to Gintrac or Carennac to stroll and watch the last hint of light fade to darkness on the ocher stone. By this time it would be midnight and we would lapse into long silences, looking up at the beautiful sky filled with stars, and stars, and shooting stars. This state of bliss happened many, many times."

7

GONE FISHING

Before Marilyn and Charles arrived for their second visit the following year, I wanted to try my hand at fishing. Fishermen are a common sight on the Dordogne. They stand poised like statues in the currents of the river. During my first few years at the house, they remained more or less in my peripheral vision. Then, for some reason—perhaps I felt more settled and attentive—I suddenly thought, Why don't *I* go fishing? It would be another way of participating in the life in the country; I would be part of the picture. And what a treat it would be to bring home a fresh catch and pop it in the frying pan. I'd fished as a kid in the Missouri Ozarks, but that had been in a lake—and it seemed so long ago. Trout fishing, involving fly casting in river waters, was another matter. Lessons were in order.

So, prior to the spring trip, I signed up for a weekend fishing course with the Orvis company, which was held at the Eldred Preserve, in upstate New York. This was completely an academic exercise—the aim was not to catch fish but to master technique. After an extremely tedious day of casting, recasting, and more recasting, I was anxious for the real thing, which I was convinced would be more enthralling than merely practicing, like playing a Chopin sonata would be after hours and hours of Bach finger exercises. But of course I had to have the proper equipment. It was like anything else—biking, running; if you were really going to get into it with any degree of seriousness, you had to be properly outfitted. The accoutrements of fishing were immensely appealing and gave me a sense of authenticity, of transformation. Through an Orvis mail-order catalog, I laid out a couple of hundred dollars for rod and reel, vest, waders, flies, leaders, and—even more irresistible—polarized glasses and a shirt with the image of a handsome trout in a graceful, leaping-for-the-fly arch. I shipped the entire regalia to the closet-size Carennac post office to await my arrival. GARDEZ JUSQU'À L'ARRIVÉE DU CLIENT, I marked the packages, envisioning Monsieur the Postmaster, a pasty-faced and stoical gentleman, scrutinizing the boxes. *"Qu'est-que c'est que ça?"* I could imagine him muttering to the deaf walls. *"Comme c'est ennuyeux!"*

When I arrived at Pech Farguet and considered the foreign waters, I experienced a momentary loss of confidence. I decided it would be wise to engage a guide for my first time out on the river. At a sporting-goods shop in St-Céré, I found the very man: the young salesperson himself, who seemed not the least surprised at my request. The next afternoon we drove to a spot on the river, where, he wagered, the trout were running. Gearing up—he unabashedly took a pee before pulling on his waders—we descended the bank and waded into the shallow river.

Here, my real education began. Lesson one: how to walk in the river. The bottom was a bed of rocks coated with an incredibly slippery greenish-brown film. I was making extremely slow progress. The proper way to go forward, he showed me as I careened and toppled, was to pick up each foot all the way out of the water—rather like a high-stepping marcher—and set it down in a firm manner. I tried, but my feet, encased in the weighty waders, felt like tree stumps. I tottered after him, like a child taking its first steps. Once we arrived at a spot midriver, lesson two began: casting. I know all about this, I thought, gritting my teeth but holding my peace. Not so. The Orvis people had favored an overhead casting method, reserving a side method for ticklish spots where shoreline brush and trees would interfere from behind. My French guide relied principally on the side technique. Thus passed another afternoon of casting, recasting, and more recasting in this fashion. From time to time he deftly changed both of our flies—which, just watching, seemed as exasperating to me as trying to thread a needle without my glasses—explaining the necessity of imitating the types of mites in the air. To make the fish feel at home. The subtle differences between flies and their relationship to the local insects could have been the subject of a doctoral dissertation. I could see the near-invisible army of infinitesimal insects adrift over the river, but as far as I could tell, they lacked any distinct character. I felt the nausea of defeat. Fishing, which I'd thought of as something of a carefree activity, was turning into a tedious, discouraging exercise. Catching trout was less a matter of fun and luck than of science and seasoned skill. Yet I tried to buoy my spirits up as we headed—troutless—back to the house through the twilight. It was a beginning.

On the way I stopped by the Bézamats. Monsieur, who is attuned to the smallest details of his surroundings, could not restrain his curiosity. What was the fishing gear doing in the backseat of my car? An account of my fishing expedition—and my hopes to pursue this endeavor—was met with a long pause, the raising of the cap, revealing the patch of white forehead where the sun never reached, the scratch of the head—his typical gestures of confoundment. A complicated thought process was playing across his face. I would never catch any fish this way, he pronounced. Or, on the off chance that I did—and his rocking hand, in a sort of *comme çi comme ça* gesture, indicated that this was unlikely—the fish would be coming from polluted water. Or, at least, water that was not as pure as in former days.

If I wanted to catch trout, in the finest water, he knew the place. He accompanied this declaration with a dramatic landing-the-fish pantomime: hands joined as on a fishing rod, a moment's hesitation, then a jerking of his arms over his shoulder. He repeated the gesture with accelerating speed: *whoosh, whoosh, whoosh.* Point made, he came to a standstill. Would I care to go along with him Sunday afternoon to catch some fish? Marilyn and Charles had arrived the day before and planned to indulge in the three-hour Sunday ritual feast at the restaurant in Loubressac. I told them to save room for some trout that evening.

The afternoon was full of promise: sunshine, blue sky, a ruffling breeze in the air. I arrived at the Bézamats at the stroke of two o'clock, the time agreed upon for our rendezvous. When I pulled into the yard beside the garage,

Monsieur ambled down the outside stairs, followed by Madame, in a flowery short-sleeved dress, trailed by the twins. The girls admired, with suppressed giggles, my trout T-shirt. I began to unload my gear from my car, when Monsieur informed me that this wouldn't be necessary. That was puzzling, and a little annoying. Perhaps, I thought fleetingly, grouchily, we were only meant to watch Monsieur fish.

We piled into the car, a somewhat dilapidated Citroën, the two girls and me wedged in the backseat. I had brought a map in order to track the secret Bézamat "fishing hole." We drove for nearly a half hour, meandering along back roads, through open country and thick sun-dappled forest. Eventually, we turned onto a narrow dirt road that wound downhill. At the bottom of the hill, Monsieur Bézamat stopped the car. There were a number of other cars parked beside a large shed. Kati and Françoise bolted. Madame Bézamat hoisted herself out and smoothed her dress, as if she was about to greet her hostess at a dinner party.

A hefty woman came forward and babbled away with the Bézamats as if they were old acquaintances. She had a deep harelip, which may or may not have been why I could barely understand a word she said. Madame Bézamat retired to a nearby lawn chair, where a group of women, with whom she was apparently friendly, had congregated. The rest of us—Kati and Françoise reined in by their father—followed the broad back of the woman to the shed, where she presented us with fishing poles, of the rudimentary sort Huck Finn would have used, and a tin of worms. The mystery was beginning to unravel before me, but my brain was still probing: what's going on? I trailed Monsieur, who had headed off on a tiny footpath.

We quickly arrived at two concrete pools, each the length of a cows' trough, where clouds of trout swarmed and darted in unison, as if controlled by an invisible switch, from one end to the other.

It was a trout hatchery.

This was outrageous.

Yet what was I to do but follow suit? Monsieur and the twins were hastily threading worms on their hooks. Recoiling, I skewered a worm on mine. I dropped in my line and the bait was instantly snatched by a trout—they actually seemed to be in a *competition* to get hooked. We were all bringing in fish as fast as we could hook the worms, in the exact manner of Monsieur's pantomime. I left the kill to Monsieur, who would swiftly thwack the fishes over the head with a short wood plank. Within a matter of minutes we had an adequate supply for all our dinners.

Back in the shed, the woman weighed our trout, and we paid accordingly. It was quite reasonable. Monsieur Bézamat collected Madame and we all bundled into the car for home.

What had Monsieur been thinking of when he suggested the outing? I thought peevishly. That I wanted fish, of course. But not the challenge, the sport, the satisfaction of the catch? I was deflated. He, on the other hand, was elated, to have shared with me his foolproof fishing grounds. Marilyn and Charles read my disappointment when I returned. "Kind of like going strawberry picking," Charles said, chuckling. I had to admit, though, as I rested my fork and knife on my plate that evening, that it was probably the best trout I'd ever eaten: the flesh was pink, as rosy as a salmon's, and full of flavor.

After this episode, my interest in fishing waned. Some

things take hold; others are passionate but passing fancies. Somehow I could never muster the enthusiasm again: all that gear, all the effort just to get situated in the water, those impossible flies and the dismaying know-how required. I wanted more instant gratification. Monsieur Bézamat's version certainly provided that, but it lacked the sense of sport. Now the equipment is stashed away, a vague reminder of diminished expectations, unrealistic dreams. I don't even wear my trout T-shirt; I don't feel I've earned the right to. I've thought of asking at the sports shop in St-Céré if I could trade in my fishing pole for something else. But I can't think what it would be just now. And, then, *on ne sait jamais*—you never know.

On the way to the "fishing" expedition, I had mentioned to Monsieur that there was something peculiar in my house. In the tiny utility closet adjacent to the fireplace in the main room, I had noticed a sticky substance, like thick buckwheat honey, running from the ceiling of the closet to the floor. It had a decidedly unpleasant odor.

Monsieur promised to stop by the next day. He arrived in the late afternoon, along with Madame, Kati, and, not to be excluded from the adventure, Bobbie the dog. Marilyn and Charles had gone off on a sightseeing expedition. Monsieur entered the house in his customary fashion, stepping out of his shoes without skipping a beat. He is totally unconscious of this habit and of the oddness of his padding about my house in his stocking feet. At first I thought it was perhaps a behavioral tic instilled in him as a boy by his mother and reinforced by his wife, who didn't want their floors muddied. It certainly had nothing to do with the Japanese ritual of leaving shoes at the door to acknowledge the sacredness of the interior. Later, I discovered the practical purpose for this habit, when I became infested with some type of chigger after a walk in the woods. The local pharmacist I'd consulted explained that you had to have a pair of both outdoor and indoor shoes—never should the outdoor shoes, which could carry insects, be worn indoors.

Madame ensconced herself on the patio. Kati lay on the grass while Bobbie charged her, yapping at her heels and head, as if she were fallen prey. Monsieur inspected the problem closet. He drew an index finger across the brown substance and smelled it, wrinkling his nose in distaste.

"Les toilettes marchent?" he asked me.

Mais oui, no problem with the toilet.

He summoned his wife and ordered her to stand by the closet. He ascended the staircase to the upstairs bathroom, which is located directly above the closet. He flushed the toilet.

Madame turned an ear to the open closet, where the sound of water could be heard gushing through the pipes.

"Ça marche, Charles. C'est beang," Madame shouted shrilly with her twist of patois.

He flushed the toilet again.

Once again, gushing, gurgling water flowed cleanly through the pipes.

"Ça marche, Charles. C'est beang," Madame called out at a higher pitch, as if loudness added credibility.

Monsieur descended the stairs, looking defeated and mystified, hat tipped back to allow his fingers to massage his brain.

It was a Monday, France's day off—small chance of getting a plumber. Monsieur Prysbil, the elderly plumber who was responsible every fall for turning off the water in my house, was known to take a siesta at this time, after his full complement of wine at lunch. (Prysbil was taken periodically to a nearby clinic for his drinking problem.) Marc Bru, Madame Servais's nephew, who lived about ten minutes away, was mentioned, but he was away visiting in-laws.

"*Mais, ça marche, Charles,*" Madame repeated.

"*Oui, ce n'est pas la toilette,*" I chimed in.

Monsieur ignored us, carrying on what appeared to be a debate with himself.

He instructed us to stand by and wait for his return. Off he went in the car, without explanation. I offered Madame a cool drink and we sat on the patio. I'm normally a person who likes to feel in control, and at times like this in France I feel the reins slipping away. Okay, I say, just wait and see. I mentioned to Madame that I hadn't known that Marc Bru was a plumber, and that perhaps it would be best if he took over Prysbil's duty at my house. Madame wholeheartedly agreed. Prysbil, she said, was *un voleur* who overcharged me.

A sputter of gravel on the road and Monsieur was back, with a tall ladder strapped to the roof of the car— and his son, Serge. They braced the ladder on the base of the patio, resting it against the roof beneath the bathroom window. Monsieur climbed the ladder, followed by Serge. They began to turn over the tiles of the roof, one by one, sniffing at each opening. Madame and I stood, gazing upward like two children at a puppet show. Then, suddenly, they came to a halt at a spot directly above the closet.

"*Qu'est-ce que c'est?*" I asked Madame.

She wheezed, which I took to mean not to ask questions.

From high above Monsieur called down, *"C'est la bête,"* spitting out the words as if he'd bitten a rotten apple.

I knew whereof Monsieur spoke. The beast had a history at the house.

The past summer, when Marilyn and Charles had visited, they had had a run-in with the animal—and better them than I, I'd said when I heard the unnerving tale. In the middle of the night, they had heard what sounded like a one-man band in the kitchen, with a banging of pots and pans and a clatter of dishes. Charles had bounded out of bed and descended the stairs on tiptoe, Marilyn in his wake. He had flicked on the light, and there, poking out from under the stove, was a bushy tail, waving like a little flag.

It was at this rather alarming moment, Marilyn confided in me, that she realized a radical difference between herself and her husband, which, she later decided, could have a profound effect on their marriage. Charles was a gentle soul, while she was a mad avenger.

"Isn't she cute?" Charles had said softly.

"Is there a gun in the house?" Marilyn had whispered wickedly, quaking.

Eventually, they had decided to return to bed (door firmly closed). What was there to do? By morning the animal had vanished.

But what animal? They had consulted Monsieur Bézamat, who brought out his illustrated animal book and pointed to a *martre*, which resembled a ferret.

When I arrived the next fall and stopped by the Bézamats for the keys, Monsieur announced proudly that he had shot and bagged an example of this beast. He led me around to the back of the house. He'd saved it to show me. I didn't look too closely at the matted mass of fur in the plastic sack, swarming with flies and maggots. Looking self-satisfied, he recounted, in dramatic fashion, its demise. Checking on my house at the end of summer, he had met up with Hironde, who had come by to trim the grass. When they spotted the beast, Bézamat went to fetch his gun. Hironde chased the animal to the other side of the house (a role Bézamat now played in the stance of a charging bull). Then he, Bézamat (now playing himself, the star of the show), followed with gun poised. *Pow, pow*, went the gun (Bézamat as gun, exploding like a popcorn popper). *"Eh, voilà!"*

I was secretly unimpressed. One *martre*? How different from, say, killing a single squirrel? Surely, there were more where it came from. The *bête* under the roof at this very moment was probably a cousin.

For the next hour—time I'd planned to spend putting together a *salade niçoise* for dinner—Monsieur and Serge hacked away at the insulation and substructure of the roof over the closet. The animal, who had holed up for warmth under the eaves, had apparently dropped down into a limbo region between roof and closet ceiling. It had become trapped and died.

Monsieur Bézamat and Serge suddenly shouted in triumph. The animal had been freed to drop below, into the closet. Madame and I rushed into the house.

I now know the stench of death. It is as much an assault to the senses as a physical blow. I only glanced at the scattered remains of the corpse, unidentifiable as any form of life. Madame and I reeled outdoors, gagging. Monsieur and Serge rushed into the house—everyone was moving frantically, as if there was a fire. Within minutes, they ran out, with a garbage bag between them. Madame and I returned, not without reluctance, to sweep up the rest of the debris—shards of the closet ceiling and fragments of roofing. We all stood for a moment on the patio, huffing from the exertion. Monsieur dusted his palms together in a gesture of good riddance. Serge, his usual taciturn self, was packing up the ladder. We called it a day.

The faint trace of death lingered. I took a tin of tuna fish, a wedge of bread, a tomato to eat out of hand, and a bottle of wine to the patio. I was famished.

Marilyn and Charles commiserated when they returned to the scene of destruction. "We'll think about the damage tomorrow," Charles said.

8

UNINVITED GUESTS

All God's creatures habitually hibernate in the house over the winter. When I close up the house, I imagine a little chorus in the woods: "She's going, tra-la, she's gone, ta-ta, let's get a move on." I'm now primed for Monsieur Bézamat's tales—there's usually a *martre* episode—when I arrive in the spring. Three years ago in May, when I picked up the keys, he seemed particularly perturbed. This needed an on-site explanation; he insisted on following me to the house.

Monsieur Bézamat saves supporting evidence of any unruly goings-on at the house in my absence until he sees me in person; it makes for a more dramatic account. Leading me to the fireplace, he pointed to *"caca"*—a word I don't generally hear or use but instantly grasped. The *caca* was hardened and slightly moldy. He had preserved it, as a detective would the fingerprints of a crime, in its original position on the hearth. He pointed to the far corner of the room. More *caca* had been discovered there. But this wasn't the end of the trail.

"*Permettez-moi?*" he asked, heading stocking-footed, stealthily as Poirot, for the stairs. I followed on his heels to the bedroom.

"*Voilà!*" he exclaimed, with questionable triumph. He pointed to two feathers on the bed. Two feathers. The import of this didn't register. Then he steered me to the waist-high chest of drawers beneath the small opaque-glass window. Five feathers (he counted them for me, in a dramatic fashion). Then he pointed out that the wooden frame around the window had been eaten away. This added up to a real puzzle, he said, piercing in his gaze. The *caca* was the size and shape of an *hibou*'s (the pleasingly onomatopoeic name for an owl). And Hironde had testified to sighting one sitting on the roof. But how could the bird have come down the chimney on its own to deposit its feathers in the room? Or could a *martre* have attacked the bird and carried its feathers in its bloody mouth into the house? The gnawed wood was the work of a *martre*. Monsieur related his findings with gravity and thoroughness, suggesting some long winter evenings spent on the problem.

I took all this in with the helpless ignorance of a city person, grasping for a meaningful response. Could the *caca* possibly be that of a *martre*? I proposed, straining for some logic. The *caca* seemed impressively large for that of a bird, even a big owl. This discussion, which might have struck me as decidedly coarse in English, seemed rather innocuous in French.

No, Monsieur declared, the *caca* could not be that of a *martre*. That was the rub. And what of the feathers? he grilled me. Bearing in mind, he said, adding another layer of complexity, that an owl would not eat wooden molding. That was the work of a *martre*.

I was struggling with some ridiculous mental images. Of an owl fluttering down the chimney like the Holy Ghost, doing his business, and hip-hopping up the stairs to the bedroom. Or of a little weasel-like *martre* boxing with an owl on my bed, tossing the dead bird out the window and chowing down on the window frame. The whole thing was a muddle.

What was to be done? My usual question. Clearly, the frame of the window had to be repaired. Monsieur suggested an *ébéniste*, a kind of carpenter.

I put the matter on hold for several days. How to shape the problem in terms that would seem less than lunatic to an *ébéniste*? Eventually, I decided to see one, a Monsieur Ribeiro, but not without some hesitation. I'd had on-and-off dealings with him during a two-and-a-half-year period over the agonizing construction of a picnic table.

The patio outside the house is diminutive. Seating was provided by a sorely weathered postage-stamp-size table and rickety chair left from the Pinckney days. In the spring of 1988, I decided that I would use the patio more often if I had a decent table where I could have alfresco lunches and dinners, with the valley at my feet. For years I had done nothing to dramatically change the house, which in fact needed little by way of improvement. It also felt imbued with the Pinckneys' presence, and I had been reluctant to do anything contrary to what they might have wanted. Only gradually did I begin to make a few small changes. I purchased new hand-painted dishes in a charming French faience pattern, replacing the Pinckneys' chipped Chinese set. I commissioned the plumber Prysbil, who also did custom-made wrought-iron work—he thought of himself as something of an *artiste*—to build a small railing for the balcony outside the doors of the living room, which, according to Mr. Pinckney's original drawings, had been intended but left unfinished. As the balcony stood, it was no more than a useless concrete slab jutting out over the valley—a precarious perch. At the time of my purchase I wrote the Pinckneys to inquire why they'd decided against the railing—as if I needed their permission. Mrs. Pinckney wrote back to say they preferred the sense of "dining in the trees." The picnic table, then, represented a major addition.

I spotted Monsieur Ribeiro's display room on the road to the nearby village of Vayrac and asked Monsieur Hironde if he was reliable. *"Il est Portuguais,"* was his noncommittal reply. His xenophobia seemed unconscious and not the least bit mean-spirited. He seemed to be suggesting that Ribeiro was in a category (nonnative) that defied such judgment, like a wife saying of her mother-in-law, "She has her ways." (Monsieur Ribeiro subsequently told me that he had lived in this part of France for nearly forty years, after coming to the country as a young boy.)

I met Monsieur Ribeiro, a large-boned man with broad features and a friendly, if slightly cloying manner, at his workshop. He had the offputting habit of standing in uncomfortably close proximity during conversation; his face loomed within inches of mine. I took a step backward and described the type of picnic table I wanted: a plain, solid redwood table with benches (we'd had one of this type in our backyard that had endured all my years of growing up). He pointed to a table that met my description—one of his best, attractive yet durable. It would cost much more than I'd planned to spend, but I reasoned that after all, this would be a table custom-made to fit a particular area. He requested that I pay him half the amount at the outset and the remainder when the table was completed. He agreed to stop by the house the next morning to take measurements.

He didn't show up. When I stopped by his workshop later in the day, he explained, without apologies, that he'd been delayed on another project. His manner was so gentle, I couldn't be annoyed. We made another appointment for the next morning. He arrived in his truck an hour late, oblivious of his rudeness. Being a punctual person, I am fairly intolerant of tardiness, but I restrained myself from commenting because I wanted his cooperation. He was enraptured by the wonderful view. What a pleasure it would be to eat outdoors, he said, gesticulating as if the table were already in place. I showed him where the table should go, tucked into the corner of the patio, with the stone wall at the back to take advantage of the view. He made some preliminary sketches and took exact measurements. He reassured me that the table would be rock solid and bolted to the wall so that there would be no possibility of theft (this had not occurred to me, since I'd never had any problems along that line). I was impressed with his thoroughness. The table would be completed by the time I came back in the fall.

In October, I drove lickety-split from the Bézamats to the house. No table. I bristled. He had had all those months to finish it. What could have delayed him?

What had delayed him, Monsieur Ribeiro explained when I stopped at the shop, was that he had had doubts about some specifications, and had hesitated to go ahead without my approval. What if he'd got it wrong; I would have been very unhappy, no? He arrived the next morning, only a half hour late, and we reviewed all the particulars.

I was harboring a slim hope that he could undertake the work while I was there, but no, he was up to here (hand under chin) with orders. May, then. May it would be.

May, and no table. I was seething. How could he string me along like this? The weather was perfect! I could be enjoying the patio. It was just a simple picnic table! What could be so complicated?

What was so complicated, Monsieur Ribeiro explained, was that he had had a serious accident in his workroom. We were standing there at the time. He demonstrated—slapping his forehead and reeling backward—how a part of a heavy machine had flown off and struck him. He'd had a severe concussion and had been hospitalized in Toulouse. He did look a bit pale; he'd lost a little weight. Something of his usual ebullience was gone, and his smile was wan. I felt my anger forestalled, my arguments deflated. I expressed my sympathy over his accident. The table, he promised, would be installed by the time I returned in the fall.

The following September, it was, at last, THERE. There, in capital letters, because in the context of my dollhouse-sized patio, it had all the monumentality of a luxury ocean liner. The original plan for something rustic and simple had taken on grandiose dimensions in Monsieur Ribeiro's mind. What was now in place was a massive table—the sort you see in public parks—with four-inch-thick planks and brass studs the size of a French franc. How had it assumed these proportions?

I dropped my luggage at the door and immediately tested the table. It was, indeed, anchored to the stone wall—this table was going nowhere. A person had to high-step over the thick wooden slabs connecting the benches to the table and sidle awkwardly into the seat. It was like mounting a horse in a tight stall. The table was chest high, so if I rested my elbows on top, they winged out at shoulder level. Even more troubling, the table was on a slant, causing the vista to be dizzily skewed. I had visions of dinner plates slowly creeping away from the person eating from them and guests muttering about disappearing eating utensils. To climb out of the table took as much dexterity as getting in—God forbid you should forget the salt! But I buried my sickening disappointment. It had been such an arduous feat getting the table. I could live with it, couldn't I?

The following spring, when I'd gotten some distance from it, I thought not. Even though I'd paid Monsieur Ribeiro, the result was unacceptable. When I visited his workshop to explain the problem, he agreed to stop by the house that afternoon. I invited him to sit at the table and withheld comment as he struggled with his large frame to sit down—or should I say climb aboard? He sat with a self-important rise and fall of his shoulders, looking mildly satisfied. Then I pointed out the slant, the impossible height for comfortable dining, the disorienting view. He didn't disagree. Nor did he agree. But he said he would make some slight alterations—these were not serious problems—and it would be perfect when I returned in the fall.

Need I say that the repairs had not been made in the fall?

This time Monsieur Ribeiro was not at his workshop. His son—the resemblance around the eyes and mouth was too strong for him to be anything else—seemed to be in charge. His father, he said, continued to have problems resulting from his accident and wasn't able to work to full capacity. I explained the problem, and he said he would see to it immediately. He arrived within an hour, with a young helper. It was no small job to lower the table and set it at an even level on the rough, irregular stone surface. It had to be unbolted, measured and recut, then reassembled. It took hours. When it was completed, I slid in comfortably and sat down. Perfect, it was perfect. After they left, I brought out the cheeses and *pâté*, bread and wine, and basked in the sunshine. Food, my mother always said, just tastes better outdoors.

Despite my problems with him, Monsieur Ribeiro was incontestably a fine craftsman; a more solid table you couldn't ask for. Thus, I assumed the job of repairing the window frame would be a snap. After I greeted him at his workshop—his health apparently restored—I crept up on my reason for visiting him, blathering in general about the problem of animals in the house over the winter. Then I reached the final hurdle, the nonsense about the *martre* or the *hibou*, whatever—the as-yet-to-be-determined culprit. I drew a breath. A window molding needed replacement, I announced, skidding to a conclusion.

"*Ha!*" Monsieur Ribeiro roared in my face. The *martre/hibou* issue seemed to have struck some chord, as if he, too, had suffered a similar outrage.

When he and his son arrived the following day, they studiously examined the window frame. Mystified, they asked for details. I passed on the few clues I had, producing the feathers (I was getting like Monsieur Bézamat in my old age). Monsieur Ribeiro was uncharacteristically subdued, stumped. "*Martre, hibou,*" he muttered. I was frankly relieved just to let the matter lie. Then, with a shrug of his shoulders, he said that the solution was to cover the window with a sheet of waterproof board. A simple solution, but a sound one. Since the window was opaque and provided the faintest light (I relied on the other window for this as well as for a view of the valley), nothing would be lost by covering it up. The cover would serve as a sort of seal against animals and the elements. I hesitated only a moment. It was aesthetically distasteful, but I could keep the curtains closed.

Seizing the occasion, I asked Monsieur Ribeiro if, at the same time, he would cut a bed board for me, since my mattress was not firm enough. *D'accord.* He took careful measurements of both the window frame and the bed.

In the morning, the Ribeiros were back. In minutes, the window was sealed up. The bed board, however, proved to be a more complicated undertaking, starting with a great deal of huffing and puffing to get it up the tiny, angled staircase. Then, to my dismay, when they slid it onto my bed frame, it was inches short all the way around. I was beginning to have serious doubts about Monsieur Ribeiro's skills with a tape measure. Until he explained the problem: this particular board was the only size, of the thickness I'd demanded, that he'd had on hand. But it wouldn't do, I countered, since the mattress would extend over the edge all the way around. He looked resigned to this fact. But now, he said with immense regret, the bed board would have to wait on a fresh supply of wood so that he could cut it to my specifications. I knew what this meant: sometime, far down the road, I would have my bed board. Maybe by fall, certainly by spring.

I drew the curtains across the board on the window—and on the unsolved mystery. *Hibou* or *martre*, we would never know.

9

BREAKDOWN

One of the advantages of the house is using it as a base to explore *la France profunde*, as the French refer to the countryside. Often I split a vacation between a visit to the house and a sojourn to a particular area in another part of the country. It's immensely satisfying simply to toss a nightgown and a toothbrush in a bag for an overnight stay at a not-too-distant inn. A further advantage of *my* house is that I can go any which way: farther south to the Basque country, east to the Auvergne, north to the Loire, southeast to Provence. . . . The only problem is that I have to rely on rental cars, and this can be expensive.

In April 1990, I spent a week in Brittany. I'd been lured to that part of the country by what I'd read about its whitewashed villages, rocky inlets, and coastal cliffs rising above crashing waves; of its enduring legends (King Arthur searched for the Holy Grail in the forests of central Brittany); of its fierce independence (staunchly clinging to the Breton language, which is closer to Welsh than to French). It sounded like a mystical place. I limited myself to a stretch of the Western coast, starting with the serene little town of St-Brévin-les-Pins. For dinner and lodging, I relied on my on-the-road Bible, the *Logis de France*, which is reissued each year. In order for a hotel-restaurant to qualify for the guide—and post the cheery green-and-yellow *Logis de France* sign on its exterior—it must offer reasonable rates and regional cuisine. The guide includes regional maps, pinpointing the location of each *logis*, which are usually family-run affairs. At a glance, you can see that the country is riddled with them—and once you've keyed into the *logis*, the little green-and-yellow sign catches your eye everywhere. Since I don't travel in high season, I often simply call ahead from one evening to the next for a reservation; at times I haven't even called ahead, when I'm not sure where I'll wind up at the end of the day, and have never had a problem finding lodging. This is a great comfort, banishing worry about finding a place for the night in unfamiliar territory.

Vannes, a pretty cobbled town, had some sophisticated shops, a cut above the norm in this low-key part of the country. I dawdled for the afternoon and bought a dress, a rare indulgence. It had a brilliantly colored design and would call for a special occasion—I had to take a walk around the block to persuade myself that this flamboyant whim would be in fact a reasonable choice. My Brittany dress it would be. That night I stayed in Quiberon at Le Neptune, where my room had a panoramic view of the bay.

On the road past Carnac, on an appropriately gray, somber day, I spotted some of the curious, eerie menhirs

I'd read about. The giant stones, some weighing up to three hundred and fifty tons, were like swells in the earth, here as if created by a colony of giant moles. In fact, it was the Druids, members of ancient religious orders and regarded as pagan magicians in Christian legends, who assembled them from 5000 to 2000 B.C. Their meaning in ancient rituals has yet to be understood and their presence in the natural landscape is disturbing and haunting. Tourists were walking about the terrain, heads down in a studious perusal, as if they could uncover the mystery. I drove on, satisfied with the sight from the car.

In Quimperlé I happened on to a pint-size six-table *crêperie* near the cathedral for lunch, where a woman in historic Breton dress was turning out the battery of orders for *galettes* from her station near the front window. It was a fascinating example of the art of *crêpe* making. The batter was contained in a deep yellow bucket beside her. Across the top of the bucket was a wooden plank to hold utensils and a hole carved out for a measuring cup. In front of her were two large gas-heated griddles, which she continually adjusted (every time the door opened, a blast of cool air came in). She would dip a cloth-covered sponge in melted butter to coat one griddle. Then she poured in a cupful of batter and smoothed it out with a wooden spatula. Within seconds the batter would begin to bubble. She would peek at the underside and, if she was satisfied, flip the *crêpe* on its undone side to the second griddle. With dazzling sleight of hand, she then started another *crêpe* on the first griddle. Immediately, she would spread the filling on the cooked *crêpe*, fold it, flip it over and back again, and glide it onto a plate. For the family at the next table, it was chocolate and raspberries; then, for me, *gruyère*. Her *crêpe* making went on and

on in a balletic sequence, without pause. I was mesmer-
ized and would like to have lingered, but I had gobbled
up my *crêpe*—one goes down very quickly—and people
were backed up at the door waiting for tables.

After that, *crêpes* became my regular lunch fare. For
breakfast, I discovered a delicious pastry called *kouign-
amann* (the pronunciation of which I never quite mastered), a Breton specialty that has a crisp exterior and
a buttery, almost creamy interior. I scanned bookstores
for a regional cookbook with the recipe and eventually
found it in a slim paperback lyrically titled *Balades
Gourmandes, 77 recettes de la Bretagne et des pays de la
Loire*. Among its charming illustrations of old posters
and photographs is one of an elderly peasant woman
plucking chickens. A skinny naked chicken, like one of
those rubber versions you sometimes see in a circus
clown's act, is nearly swallowed up in the depths of her
capacious lap, with its neck dangling over one knee.
She is gesturing with an outstretched arm, an animated
expression on her face, regaling someone out of sight
with a story. I stared at this photo time and again, trying
to imagine what her tale could be. Just scanning the recipe for *kouign-amann*, I could see why it was so outra-
geously good. It called for twice as much butter as flour!
The recipe is time-consuming, requiring four *tours*, fold-
ings and rollings of the dough, each followed by fifteen-
minute chillings, to create flaky layers as in a croissant. I
plan to try it at home some Sunday morning, but I know
that, food being more than a question of taste, I'll never
be able to replicate it. I won't be seated in a tiny village
café by the sea as the sun does battle with the early-
morning fog and the brisk, briny air has caused me to
work up a keen appetite. Some things just don't translate.

For dinner, I had nothing but seafood—oysters, mussels,

lotte, rouget, lobster—and whatever dessert featured apples, usually a warm *tarte aux pommes,* once with the
wonderful cold contrast of a scoop of honey-nutmeg ice
cream.

On the outskirts of Pont-Aven, Gauguin's stomping
grounds, there is the Trémalo Chapel, whose sixteenth-
century wooden Christ is said to have inspired the artist's
Yellow Christ. It paled, of course, next to the shocking
egg-yolk figure in the painting. Even more fascinating,
though utterly nondescript, was the tiny sixteenth-century
chapel at Nizon. When I entered, no one was there. It
was so still that I thought I could hear the flutter of angels' wings, or was it just the wind at the door? There
was little by way of ornamentation, save for some ancient
and worn painted wooden statues, with their blessed innocent faces staring fixedly into space. Here were price-
less antiquities, completely unguarded and vulnerable.
Anyone could have made a heist. I daringly reached up—
what if someone caught me in the act!—and touched the
craggy, timeworn cheek of one.

From there, I drove a short distance away to the fascinating small fishing village of Kescott, with its cluster of
Hansel-and-Gretel-type thatched houses. I surreptitiously
peeked inside as I strolled by; it would be like living in a
dollhouse. They were probably no longer owned by fishermen, but by wealthy Parisians who stocked them with
antiques and tended their colorful flower gardens.

At this easygoing pace, the days slipped by. I had already decided to return to Brittany before I'd even left. At
the end of the coastal journey I stayed at the Hotel de la
Plage, in Sainte-Anne-la-Palud. In *La Belle France,* a
monthly newsletter to which I subscribe—I'm a complete
sucker for any guidebooks or publications relating to
France—I read that Sainte-Anne-la-Palud was reputed to

be an unhappily married Cornish princess who was magically transported to Nazareth, where she gave birth to
the Virgin Mary—a new twist on the story of my name-
sake that made me feel specially anchored to this place.

The hotel was a great rambling white house lolling at
the edge of the sea, the coastline reminiscent of Maine.
My room opened to the vista of a cove of smooth sand,
placid blue water with white curls of waves lapping at
the shore, lavender hills down the coast. I'd arrived at the
end of the world. Before dinner, I took a forty-five-minute
run inland, with views of lush green hills dotted with
cows. Farmhouses glowed in the rosy late-afternoon light.
Occasionally, in the distance, I saw a glint of sea. When
I got back, I took a luxurious bubble bath (the only time
I ever pamper myself this way is at a spiffy French hotel),
and was ready for dinner. The floor-to-ceiling windows in
the dining room, literally at water's edge, provided a
sweeping view of a motionless sea. That evening, the
other diners were a young couple with two impressively
well-behaved small children, and two older couples; together they created a gentle, comforting murmur of conversation. As dinner progressed, the light changed from a
brilliant silvery white that dramatically illuminated the
clouds to a fiery red ball sinking into the sea. Did this call
for romance? Did I wish at that moment to be sitting
with the love of my life? Yes. There are such times.

Early the next morning I took a solitary walk on the
beach. The sea was as calm as a pond. Pebbles and shells
crunched under my running shoes. I scanned the beach as
I strode along. I've collected shells from time to time but
always find that they seem uninteresting when I get them
home. Then I spied an unusual-looking rock, flat on the
bottom and rising into a pleasingly miniature boulder

shape. It was a pearly gray green, with strands and webs of white running across the surface, like the tracks of some natural force that had left its mark long, long ago. It fit handily into my cupped hand. Today it sits on my window ledge and can call back with a glance that magical place.

I packed my bag and tossed it in the front seat, with one last glance past the dunes. I resolved to come back—though I've said that before of other places. It would be when I wanted a retreat, to drop out of the world for a space of time.

Locronon, a tiny medieval town. Châteaulin, Carhaix-Plouguer, Rostrehen, Pontivy, Josselin. I whispered the names of the towns as I drove along, softer than the guttural *ac* villages of the Lot: Carennac, of course, and Vayrac, Gintrac, Padirac, Souillac, on and on. I had once asked Charles, who is a history buff, why there is a proliferation of *ac*s in my region. Charles's answer to such questions are always elaborate.

Ac, Charles explained, is a shortening of the Latin ending *acum*, which was affixed to a name to indicate "place of" or "villa of." The form appeared when names started to be written down in Latin, usually in lists of parishes or in monastic charters. The earliest records are from the ninth century, but probably that is only the tail end of a process of writing down names in Roman Gaul that goes back to the era just after Caesar's conquest (about 50 B.C.). The form *acum* or *iacum* was applied to both personal names and to existing Celtic places. Thus Pauliac or Tauriac suggest the villas of Paulus or Taurus. Carennac, on the other hand, suggests "the place of the quarried stone," based on a possible Celtic root *carenna*. The place-names of the old Haut-Quercy region, he postulated, may be among the least affected by historical change in all of France. Neither the Visigoths (in the Garonne Valley) nor the Francs (north of the Vezère) contributed much settlement to the area, and so antique forms of place-names are more common there.

As I traveled inland, the *crêperies* tapered off. Eventually, I reached Chartres for an overnight stay before going on to Paris. In the afternoon I revisited the cathedral I'd seen many years ago. For some reason—perhaps because it had struck me the first time as so amazingly intricate and jewellike—it had seemed *smaller* then. Now it soared. That night after dinner I watched a television program in my room, a sort of musical special presenting the top hits in descending order. The range of music offered a little something for everybody. I was enraptured by one singer, a man well into his sixties, the quintessential French *chanteur*, with his squashed angling hat and dapper suit, woeful eyes under eyebrows pitched at forty-five-degree slants, like facing *grave* and *acute* accents, an ash-laden cigarette dangling from his lips. Despite the cigarette, he managed to sing a song of—what else?—unrequited love. After the program I turned off the light and took in a last fairy-tale view from my window of an illuminated château casting its exact upside-down reflection in the river.

I decided to skip breakfast that morning. I'd be in Paris by noon, so I could have a big lunch at the end of the journey. It was Monday morning—a bleak, cold morning typical of mercurial April—and traffic was heavy on the autoroute leading into the city. It soon began to rain, not a mild spring rain but a hard-driving, blinding torrent that showed no signs of abating. Cars and trucks (monstrous trucks that spewed sheets of water in their wake) had all turned on their headlights. I turned off the car radio in order to concentrate fully on my driving. I was in the center lane of the one-way three-lane route. Suddenly I heard a loud grinding and thumping sound, which I at first mistook for some alarming external force. Then, to my utter horror, I realized it was *me*, the car, which then began to jolt like a bucking bronco. I let up on the gas pedal immediately and managed to ease into the right-hand lane, at which point the engine died. I coasted onto the extremely narrow shoulder, the right side of the car smack against the guardrail, the driver's side nearly flush with the lane of streaming traffic. My heart raced. I turned off the motor. At least I was safely out of traffic, although in a terribly vulnerable position. I looked around me for any landmark. There was only a blurred, endless horizon, without a sign of civilization. I had no idea where I was. I studied my road map, but since I'd been confined to the featureless autoroute and hadn't been paying attention to signposts—it was going to be a straight shot, Chartres to Paris—I couldn't figure out my location. Even a rough estimate, though, indicated no outlying villages or towns.

The natural impulse, of course, was to summon help. I inched my way out of the car—I could only open the door a crack—and was instantly whipped with lashes of rain from the zooming cars and monster trucks (*poids lourds*). I stationed myself at the rear of the car and waved frantically. I felt about the size of a bug. No one stopped. No one *would* stop, I realized before long. This was the Monday morning rush to Paris. My light windbreaker was completely soaked, worthless under these conditions. I scurried back inside the car. I tried turning over the engine—please, *please*, I begged it. Stone-cold dead, without even a whimper or cough.

I was staring out the front window, trying to still my

mounting panic, when I saw—could it be?—a yellow signpost marked s.o.s. 800 m. How far would that be? My runner's standard—ten kilometers equals six miles—told me it couldn't be far. I set off at as brisk a pace as I could manage in the whipping rain. I was walking for what seemed an eternity. How far to go? The rain felt like tears streaming down my face, but I couldn't cry. If I let go, I would crumble. Suddenly a car pulled up on the shoulder behind me. I spun around and ran to whoever my savior might be. I opened the door a crack. The driver, an elegant middle-aged woman with soft curly black hair, a pert hat, and stylish suit, looked as if she had important business in Paris. Her expression, however, was motherly and concerned. She motioned me inside the car. I thanked her, rather hysterically, for coming to my aid and described the problem. She eased back onto the autoroute and shook her head regretfully; the best she could do was drop me at the SOS station. That would be *wonderful*, I exclaimed. And how did the SOS work? She explained that I simply had to push the button and respond with the number of the SOS station. That would indicate my location. Help would be on its way, she assured me.

We drove on for several minutes. How far back was the car now? I'd lost all sense of distance. Soon she pulled onto the shoulder, beside a thick steel pole—not the sort of shed or way station I'd envisioned. She reviewed the procedure: push the button, wait for the response, and speak into the receiver with the SOS number. There was the number; she pointed: 113. *Cent treize*, I rehearsed. She was *désolée* that she couldn't do more, she said, with a stricken look on her face. I felt myself reflected in her expression and knew I was a sorry sight, wet and bedraggled, and obviously distraught. I summoned all the words in my repertoire to express my gratitude.

The pole was on the far side of the guardrail. I vaulted over. *Cent treize*, I prepared myself. I pushed the steel button and waited. Almost instantly, a man's voice crackled through the small speaker—*"Allô!"* I announced the SOS number. He asked for a description of the car, the license number, and my name and address. Over the roar of the storm and hell-bent trucks, I shouted a partial response (*je suis Américaine, en route à Paris*, etc.). *"Une bonne heure,"* he said. A good hour before the truck would arrive. It was nine-twenty.

The walk back to the car took approximately fifteen minutes. I wormed inside and leaned back against the headrest. I was sopping wet and shivering with the cold. I reached into my bag and changed my drenched jacket for a sweatshirt and my sodden Rockport walking shoes for running shoes. I occupied myself with the what-ifs. If the car could be repaired right away—assuming I would be taken to some sort of garage—I could go right on to Paris and that would be the end of it. If the car couldn't be repaired, I could call the nearest Avis office (I'd arranged for the rental through a New York office of the company). They were responsible, after all. They should arrange for me to get to Paris. Or, that failing, there surely would be a train or bus into the city. I had no need of the car in Paris, so nothing would be lost by that. It would work out.

An hour passed. The rain continued in relentless whipping sheets that rocked the car. I had nothing to read, but even if I had, it would have been difficult to concentrate. I kept my eyes peeled on the rearview mirror for a sign of the tow truck. I was both fatigued and jittery—and hungry. I began to contemplate what I would have for lunch. Soup, definitely. Then maybe a big puffy omelette. A cheese omelette. Dessert. Something warm. That wonderful Breton apple tart came tantalizingly to mind. Oh, for a cup of coffee! Then I closed the curtain on this line of thought: it was making me miserable.

It was nearly eleven o'clock. Over an hour and a half. What could be the trouble? I'd been able to describe the car, but I hadn't had the license number to give the man. He'd said it was not essential, but what if that had caused a problem, after all? I could picture some small-minded individual along the bureaucratic chain claiming that nothing could be done without the license number. Give it some more time, I advised myself. *Une bonne heure.* Who knew what that really meant? Weren't the French notoriously late?

I avoided glancing at my watch too frequently. Time seemed to be moving slower and slower. My brain began to fester. How would they know in which *direction* the car was from the SOS? And how could they know how *far* I was from the station? I'd never pinpointed my exact location. But then how could I? And wouldn't they have asked? The doubts began to plague me. Maybe if they at least knew that I was in a westerly direction from the SOS, it would be helpful. Why not go back to the SOS and give them the license number this time? But I should run. What if they arrived and didn't find me at the car? Would they bypass me? I'd have to keep on the lookout for the tow truck on the way to the SOS.

Once the idea took hold, I was possessed by it. I climbed out of the car, jotted down the license number, and set off at a somewhat lumbering run through the rain. At the SOS, I bounded over the rail, pushed the button, and waited for the *allô*. I gave my name and announced that I had the license number. But before I had a chance to relay it, the sharp, splintered voice commanded, *"Retournez à la voiture!"* The message was delivered in such a militaristic and alarming manner that I was rendered speechless. This had been a mistake. I sloshed to the guardrail, leaned my stomach against it, and swung my right leg over. As I gymnastically followed with the other leg, my running shoe caught in the lip of the rail. I spun in the air and landed on my side in a twisted heap, my shoe still hooked in the rail. I lay in the gushing, mucky river of rain. For an instant, for one hopeless instant, I considered just lying there and letting go, letting the rain and the mud and my exhaustion overtake me. I can't think when I'd ever felt so defeated, so abandoned, in my life. I worked my foot loose and slowly, very slowly, rose to a standing position, testing, testing. My wrenched knee protested. Nothing was torn or broken, but I was reduced to a hobble. It was going to take me forever to get back to the car. A refrain of my father's jingled in my head—one of his little slogans for life that had an unpleasant edge to it: when the going gets tough, the tough get going.

At long last I reached the car, drenched and chilled to the bone. Could the tow truck have come and gone? I could hardly bear the thought. Stiff-legged, I eased into the car. I needed to examine my knee and was frightened of what I might find. There was a pair of slacks in my bag. My wet jeans were stiff and heavy, but I managed to wiggle out of them. The knee was angry-looking and swollen; I cupped it tenderly in my palms. The other knee, to my surprise, was bloody and bruised. I pulled on the dry slacks and wrapped my arms around myself. I glanced at my watch. Twelve-twenty. *Une bonne heure* had turned into three. I drew into myself. It was important to keep the reins. I was walking a fine line in my mind and had to stay the course. I sat, with my head back, and thought, really, of nothing at all. I'd gone past worrying anymore, past thought, past caring. Something would happen.

And so it did. In the rearview mirror I saw the miraculous, joyous sight of a tow truck! Could it be? Could it be *my* tow truck? I bounded from the car and hailed it. Sure enough, it pulled up smartly in front of the car, as if, indeed, this was its destination. A short, stocky, uniformed young man jumped from the cab and tipped his cap. I could have smothered him with hugs and kisses. I no longer cared that it had taken him half a day. The important thing was that it was over, all over. Without a word, he slid into the car and attempted to start the motor. Not a peep. He slid out, made a slitting-the-throat gesture, and said simply, in the universal language, "Kaput."

The tow truck was already loaded with one automobile mounted on the rear platform. The driver jumped into the cab to release a spare platform behind. With amazing agility and speed, he hooked up my car and reeled it onto the platform. He instructed me to climb up front into the cab of the tow truck.

The door handle was as high as my upstretched arm. I yanked on the enormous thing and managed to open the door, which was at the level of my head. I mounted the high step with my good leg and stood poised like a flamingo. Inside, crammed into the single passenger seat, was what I took to be a Japanese family: a woman with a young girl in her lap near the driver's seat and beside her her husband. Where was I meant to sit?

"Hello," I said. The Japanese gentleman nodded, a sort of curtsy. His wife looked stonily ahead. With all the aplomb I could manage—as if I were merely assuming my proper seat at the opera—I hoisted myself into his lap. I am tall and slender. He was short and squat. Not a match. I anchored myself with my arms on the dashboard. I had to bend my head slightly so as not to glance off the roof. My knee was throbbing; there was very little space for my long legs. I wriggled a bit on his lap, like a roosting hen, to ensure a better perch. It was extremely uncomfortable for everyone, but not a word of complaint. We were off.

No one spoke. Where were we going? I wondered with only mild curiosity. I didn't care, not one iota, where I was being taken. I was back in the world of the living. We rumbled along for nearly a half hour, when I began to see road signs for Paris. That lifted my spirits tremendously. That close! Could it be that the tow truck was going into Paris? I didn't ask. I just waited to see. Shortly thereafter we turned off the autoroute and onto a secondary road. The tow truck pulled up to a stop at the side. The driver craned his neck to inform me that another truck would be arriving to pick up my car. Where would I be taken? I finally stirred myself to ask.

"*Avis,*" the driver said. Aaa-vee.

That was positive news. I extracted myself—aching neck, aching back, aching knee—from the Japanese gentleman's lap. "Good-bye," I said politely, as if we'd been fellow guests at a party.

Within minutes the second truck arrived, a smaller, single-car pickup. My car was released from the large tow truck and remounted on the second, smaller one. I climbed into the front seat of the truck.

"*Où allez-vous?*" the young driver inquired eagerly

with a bright smile, as if this was simply an unexpected stop on my pleasure trip. He was boyish and thin, as if he'd grown too tall too quickly for his body. His ears stood out prominently from his head. They were the strangest ears—flat as a pancake, with no curl at the edges. Though he was slight, this gave his head a somewhat elephantine appearance, which was disturbing and endearing at the same time.

"Paris," I said.

"*Anglaise?*" he asked. The usual.

"*Non, Américaine,*" I replied, and awaited, and received, the usual ripple of surprise.

He very much wanted to come to America, he informed me. Oh, New York, it must be very exciting to live in New York. This was a familiar conversation, but now I was charmed, giddy, to be reattached to normal life.

At the Avis agency, a small building that seemed to be located on the industrial outskirts of Paris—factories and warehouses surrounded it—the car was unloaded from the pickup. I took out my belongings, congratulating myself for being a light packer, thanked my driver, and approached the desk.

I explained the problem with the car to a surprisingly jolly gentleman—surprisingly jolly, that is, for someone at an Avis complaint desk. He pulled out some official forms; this clearly was not the first such incident of its kind. He explained that, first, I would have to pay (by credit card, of course) the expenditures for the towing, but that I would be reimbursed by Avis. Second, I had the option of taking another rental car if I needed it, or—he pointed across the way—simply taking the *métro* into Paris.

The *métro*! It was right here! I was elated to be relieved

of the car. Suddenly, after the excruciating march of time since dawn, things were moving forward at an amazing clip. I signed all the papers.

Was there anywhere I could get lunch? I asked. It was nearly one o'clock. He pointed down the road.

I limped along, bobbing with my bag on the good-leg side. I entered the restaurant, a large room with Formica-topped tables and wooden chairs. It was hot and smoky, crowded and noisy. The customers were all men, obviously workers from the surrounding factories nearing the end of their lunch hour. I'd never been in such a nitty-gritty place in France and, since I was largely ignored, was relishing every minute of it. I found an unoccupied corner table and ordered a beer, never mind coffee. I wanted whatever was filling: an omelette, a *cheese* omelette, french fries. The waitress promptly brought a basket filled with a loaf of bread and butter, and I reached for it greedily.

Ravenous hunger, a state that I'd passed through a number of times since dawn, is a primitive sensation, one that I had rarely felt, I now realized. I'd never say "I'm starving!" so offhandedly again. I ate the entire loaf of bread, slathering it with butter. I was grateful for the buzz of activity around me, conscious of my foreignness and relieved to be ignored. I was riveted on food. I asked for another beer when the waitress brought the omelette and fries. They might have been the best I'd ever had. The omelette—a huge, plump mound—was cooked perfectly, the cheese mellow. The fries were crisp and greaseless. I couldn't have done better in Paris. I ate until I was satiated and finished my second beer, feeling pleasantly light-headed.

The *métro* stop was the last on the line. I still had no

precise idea where I was. I studied the subway map and
saw that I would come into Paris at Les Invalides; the fa-
miliarity of the name was immensely comforting. The ride
took nearly forty-five minutes. It wasn't until I reached a
familiar stop that I felt, finally, anchored in the world.

I checked into one of my favorite hotels in Paris, Hotel
des Marronniers, where I often stay. The desk clerk
greeted me warmly. It was four-ten. I went to my room,
dropped my bags, and collapsed on the bed—for only a
minute of thanksgiving. I drew a hot bath in the tub and
closed the door to capture the heat and steam. I eased
into the water and propped my bad leg on the ledge. I encased my knee with a hot wet towel; it probably needed
ice, but the heat felt good. I replenished the hot water,
feeling the steam fill my lungs. Finally, I wrapped myself
in a bath towel and curled up in bed. I turned on the television to find a tennis match in progress; it didn't matter
to me who was playing. This was perfect, requiring no
thought. It was a beautiful spring day in Paris, just out
my window. Normally I would have been sorry to be
missing it. Instead, I felt . . . grateful. Grateful for having
survived.

If I had been with a friend, I considered, it would have
been an entirely different experience. Human disasters, on
a small or grand scale, are always alleviated by the presence of others. But I had had no one to provide a buffer
for me in the situation. That had made all the difference.
That was the essence of the trauma. With a friend, it
would have been more bearable. It might even have provided a laugh.

One thing was sure, however: I'd had enough of
rented cars.

10

FAMILY DINNER

For years, I sought a sense of belonging in this corner of France. A feeling of anonymity—a frustrating reminder of how our sense of self depends on others—sometimes nagged at me. When I would arrive at the Bézamats, Kati and Françoise would dart to the porch and then scurry inside. *"C'est l'Américaine!"* they would shout to Mama and Papa. Bobbie would race up the steps of the porch and stand at the door yapping, his tail quivering in the air like an exclamation point punctuating their shrilling. I would wince. I didn't want to be the representative of a country. I wanted to feel individual, myself, in their eyes.

I considered that this estrangement had to do with the brevity of my visits, and that my neighbors—not only the Bézamats, but the Servais and the Salgues and the Hirondes, to an extent—subconsciously didn't seek more than a casual relationship since I had not made a deeper, more continuous investment in their world. On the other hand, there seemed to be a difference between us: Americans, more open and personal; the French, more formal and restrained. I am always curious about their lives: their opinions, their relationships, their day-to-day habits. Yet they show little curiosity about mine. I am circumscribed by their world, the world we share.

I have a recurrent fantasy of inviting all the neighbors to dinner. (I've never figured out precisely how they relate to each other, although I suspect it's not so different from the neighbors on my Brooklyn block.) In my imagining, they all gather on the patio—for an all-American barbecue. I have to explain to them what that means: hot dogs and hamburgers on toasted buns, with mustard or ketchup, or both; potato chips (no, not french fries); coleslaw with hot bacon dressing; corn on the cob—not the fodder for cattle that it's taken for in France, but sweet and dripping with melted butter; apple pie—no, not *tarte tatin*, but a mile-high pie with cheddar-cheese crust. Beer. I envision a sort of down-home *Babette's Feast*. I watch their faces. They are initially skeptical. They deign to take a bite. They stubbornly refuse comment. They eat some more. They ask for more beer. The gathering starts to feel more like a party. They ask for seconds. Score! Of course, the fantasy always comes to an abrupt halt. Where would I get the hot dogs? The corn?

So, when the Bézamats invited me to Sunday dinner—I'd known them then for seven years—I was ecstatic. My first invitation to dine *en famille*! While we'd always been on friendly and chatty terms, it had never involved socializing. At last the bridge was being crossed. We had never used each others' names in our conversations. Somehow "Madame" and "Monsieur" seemed too formal. Yet using first names seemed too familiar—I wouldn't have dared. So we skirted the issue entirely, leaving a sort of awkward hole in our conversations. It suggested to me that we hadn't quite figured out where we stood with each other: myself, the American *journaliste* (a profession the French revere); the Bézamats, country folk who took care of my house. Friendly, but not really friends. But what? This was a step forward.

Sunday dinner at the Bézamats meant noontime—the big family feast of the week. Madame Bézamat had issued the invitation as soon as I arrived to pick up the keys; this had obviously been deliberated on.

"*Alors, midi et demi,*" she said. Twelve-thirty. It was spring, and she would be occupied in the morning picking asparagus.

"*Midi et demi.*" Monsieur pointed to his watch emphatically.

Here was the opportunity to see how a country woman cooked. The Bézamats, I knew, didn't rely on village markets. Madame buys many of her supplies from the small trucks that service housewives in the countryside: the fish truck, the meat truck, the dairy truck. These vehicles, I have learned, are not a mark of "progress," as an American is apt to see it, but harken to the days when this same service was provided by horse-driven wagons. For fruits and vegetables, the Bézamats rely on their own garden.

I tried to envision what sort of dinner she would serve: hearty earthy dishes, I hoped, the recipes for which she would impart to me so that I could regale my friends at home. At precisely twelve-twenty I set off, at the last minute wrapping up a bottle of wine. Would this be correct, or only an American custom?

The Bézamats' front door opens directly into the dining

room, which is only large enough to contain a plain wooden table and six chairs. A large television set near the single window dominates the room. There is a fireplace, which burns through fall and winter, and even on a cool spring day like the one we were enjoying then. A low counter separates this room from the kitchen, which is spartan, strictly functional.

A flicker of surprise crossed their faces at the gift of wine. They made no response, leaving me wondering if they were pleased or somehow offended. Madame turned immediately to the kitchen. Monsieur put the bottle on a side cupboard and invited me to table. Serge, their son whom I'd only encountered on a few occasions, was slumped in a chair and greeted me with a perfunctory nod. Françoise was lackadaisically setting the table. She explained, with a pout, that Kati was the lucky one, waiting tables at a local restaurant on the weekends—with good tips. Monsieur poured the two of us an aperitif in a thimble-size glass. It was heavy and sweet, unidentifiable. A bowl filled with an unappetizing snarl of what looked like golden corn curls was passed around.

Madame returned with a great white tureen of soup, instructing me to serve myself first. Monsieur poured a local red wine. The cream-colored soup was vegetable, Madame replied to my inquiry. It had the texture of a purée and a bland taste. I asked which vegetables she had used.

"*N'importe,*" she said, with a shrug.

"*Pommes de terre et . . .*" I pressed.

"*Oui, carrotes, poireaux . . .*"

Had she used chicken stock? No. Simply boil the vegetables. Mash them. That was it: recipe number one. And the source of the good bread? (This was merely a polite inquiry—my automatic brain calculator had already filed it away as second to Bétaille's.) It came from the bread truck from Miers.

Françoise cleared the soup plates and replaced them with appetizer dishes. Madame then set out a platter with a giant pyramid of fat white asparagus, enough to feed twice our number. She had picked the asparagus that morning. I had always been curious about Madame's part-time labors, wondering how she was paid. Would it be indiscreet to ask? I asked, and was surprised to learn that she was paid by the hour, a more humane method, rather than by the weight of produce, although the latter would perhaps induce more of a yield. The asparagus was accompanied by a large bowl of thick store-bought mayonnaise, a combination new to me but one that I enjoyed. The asparagus were flavorful, though I struggled cutting a few woody ones. Madame explained that these had not received enough sun.

Had they ever seen or tasted green asparagus? I asked as we all took second helpings. They shook their heads in unison. In the United States, I said, in an effort to encourage discussion, green asparagus was common; the white, rare and expensive, so this was quite a treat for me. The two had entirely different tastes as well, I continued, now struggling in my mind for just what the distinction was. The white tastes more like an artichoke, I stated finally. Slight nods of the heads. No comments. I leaned back, the subject thoroughly exhausted.

What arrived next was an enormous surprise: *foie gras de canard*—duck-liver *pâté*—made by Madame herself! On the same platter were thin slices of ham that she had festively rolled into spirals like party fare pictured in a women's magazine—an effort I found strangely touching.

I oohed and aahed over the *foie gras*. This was a real honor. *Foie gras* was reserved for special occasions and holidays—and this was a generous solid block. It was luscious and rich; I applied restraint in the helpings I took, with another course surely to come. I asked where they raised the ducks, since I'd never seen any. As I spoke I realized that I had never seen any chickens either, although they had given me eggs from time to time. Monsieur Bézamat made a waving gesture above his head. Apparently there was a part of the property, farther from the house, that I had never seen.

Meanwhile Françoise replenished the breadbasket and Monsieur poured more wine. His cheeks had taken on a rosy sheen and my French was becoming more spontaneous. Serge twirled his glass on the table, staring at it with disinterest. Madame, who had been continually preoccupied with the orchestration of the dinner, was still nursing her first glass.

She had taken only the smallest helping from each dish. She bypassed the *foie gras* altogether, which reminded me of a friend's father who used to whisper "FHB" (family hold back) when dinner guests were on hand and the kids were being piggish.

The sizzle of deep-frying could be heard.

"Ne les brûle pas," Monsieur called to her, with mock gruffness. He winked at me over words that would surely rankle her. He opened another bottle of wine. Françoise arrived with a platter of sliced roast lamb. Madame followed behind with a mountain of golden *pommes dauphines*, a French version of potato puffs.

"Mon Dieu!" I exclaimed. I scooped five *pommes dauphines* on my plate and popped one in my mouth. They were heaven, delicately crisp on the outside, with crunchy

little wisps of deep-fried crust, meltingly tender on the inside. In that moment I threw restraint to the wind. I had two more helpings, of four apiece, along with a second of the well-done lamb. During the main course, conversation flagged. Everyone, in a rather trenchermanlike manner, was taken up with the food. Momentarily, I felt a chasm created by my lack of real fluency, which would have made me more comfortable, and by their provinciality.

Would Madame give me her recipe for the *pommes dauphines*? I asked her retreating back.

As Françoise cleared our plates once more, I broached the subject of cars with Serge. This roused him from his lethargy: he unwound from his slouched position. I said that given the expense of rental cars, I longed to have my own car in France. Verbalizing the wish for the first time gave it the semblance of reality. The problem, of course, I explained, was finding someone to take care of it during my long absences. Monsieur Bézamat immediately assumed that I was dropping a hint in his direction; there was no space in his garage, he said apologetically, as if an instance when he couldn't help me was distressing. Serge suggested checking out garages in the area; something could be worked out.

Françoise set a platter of cheese, small wedges of what appeared to be leftovers, in the center of the table. The breadbasket was replenished and more wine (mine was being saved) poured. Suddenly Monsieur Bézamat leaned forward and planted his elbows on the table. To my utter astonishment, he asked me to describe my home in America. My heart flip-flopped; this was the most directly personal question he'd ever asked. I launched into a detailed description of my place in Brooklyn, the relationship of this borough to Manhattan, where I worked, the river, the subway ride. My cats. It all seemed so far away. How could I make them see it, understand it? When I finished my account, he leaned back with a look of satisfaction.

When I truly thought the meal had come to an end, Madame brought forth a plain, flat prune cake. As everyone except Serge took helpings, I asked Françoise if she studied English in school. She blushed to the tips of her ears, probably anticipating my next question. Would she like to speak a little English with me? This I said in English, which reverberated oddly—out of place—in my ears. She laughed nervously and twisted her napkin. Suddenly I thought, Serge, Françoise, and Kati were unlikely to ever see America or even a world much different than the one they inhabited. They would probably marry, perhaps they would escape to a larger town, but a more foreign world would not attract them.

Monsieur brought out the walnut liqueur. We each had a tiny glass. The rest of the afternoon would be devoted to a siesta for us all, I said. Madame brought coffee.

As Françoise cleared the last of the dishes I reminded Madame of the potato-puff recipe. She shrugged. It was *très simple*. She went to a cupboard in the kitchen and set before me a box of something called Pomlesse. I was aghast, but tried not to show it. This was available in any grocery store, she said. All it needed was the addition of a little flour and water to thicken the mixture; she added an egg to transform them into *pommes dauphines*. I held the box studiously. Pomlesse, I deduced, was the catchy, singable name for "easy mashed potatoes" (*pomme*, for potato, perhaps combined with a corruption of *aise*, meaning ease). I said I would certainly try it myself.

I thanked them all effusively for the feast—we'd been at table over two hours. We stood on the porch for a moment to drink in the fresh air. As I waved to the family from the car, I was suddenly stirred, wistful. In many ways the afternoon had been a strain—there was such a gulf between our separate lives—but the Bézamats had become family to me, and I felt my solitariness in leaving them. After I got home, I took a long walk.

The next day I picked up a box of Pomlesse. It had numbered instructions with simplistic illustrations in primary colors: a hand pouring from a measuring cup, a hand stirring the mixture in a bowl, and so on. A child could easily follow them. I religiously copied each step and added Madame's egg. The consistency seemed right. I heated the oil—hot, Madame, had stressed—and dropped in globs of the mixture by heaping tablespoons. I stood and waited for the *pommes dauphines* to swell into golden puffs. They sizzled briefly. Then, through some mysterious chemistry, they rapidly disintegrated into something unrecognizable. Small granules floated around the oil and then quickly clogged together into a gummy, greasy mass.

Now, I consider myself something of a gourmet cook. I have impressed friends with sophisticated recipes; there is no challenge I wouldn't attempt in my home kitchen. This failure was trifling, of course, but all the more unacceptable for being so. I was miffed—to be thwarted by a mere package mix—and reached for the trusty loaf of bread.

Commitment

11

MY NEW CAR

During their second visit in the spring of 1989, Marilyn and Charles and I were strolling along the road by the river in St-Céré after a morning of marketing. I came to an abrupt halt before one of the cars that were parked in a bumper-to-bumper file by the stone wall.

"*That's* the car for me," I exclaimed. It was a *deux chevaux*—a two-horsepower—a classic model of Citroën, with a shiny black-and-red Art Deco design. Discontinued in 1990, the *deux chevaux* has always been the brunt of jokes among the French: open the windows if you want to pick up a little speed on the downhill—that sort of thing. As Richard Bernstein writes in his book *Fragile Glory*, the car is "a bit of the countryside priest, a bit of the nostalgic hippy, a bit of the far-out past in look."

The idea of buying a car had been brewing for a while. The continual cost of renting was one factor; the long, by-now-repetitious—and sometimes hazardous—drive from

Paris another. But I could never figure out the logistics. Where would I keep it in my absence? Who would bother turning the engine over from time to time? Who would pick me up at the train station, which was in St-Denis-Près-de-Martel (a small local train made the connection in Brive), about a fifteen-minute drive from my house? But even more significantly, did I really want to invest more in my place here, to take on more responsibility? It would be one more tie that binds. I kept dreaming.

Then, four years ago in May, I was driving (in another of my rental cars) past the garage in Bétaille, which is across the street from the bakery. It has the appearance of a sort of neglected country house—in the Midwest, come to think of it—with a weathered white painted-wood façade, plastic strips fluttering in a breeze in the open doorway, and a couple of big shaggy old dogs slumbering, like crumpled blankets, around the pumps. There is always a mysterious collection of cars parked to one side. And there it was, a shiny black-and-red *deux chevaux* glinting in the sunshine! I drove past, but my head reeled back as if it was attached by an invisible line to the car. I slowed, then crept, and finally stopped. I turned the car around and pulled into the garage.

A young mechanic in a grease-spotted blue jumpsuit was bent over the engine of a car in front of the service area. I asked if the owner was around and he pointed to the door. I waved aside the curtain of plastic strips, followed by a lumbering dog. The small room was wood-paneled. To the right was a kitchen. Perhaps it had, in fact, once been a house. Behind the desk was a squarely solid young man who was conducting a rapid-fire conversation on the phone. He raised his eyebrows in acknowledgment of my presence and raised a finger as a signal that he'd be with me momentarily. I waited, as the dog's wet muzzle nudged my hand. The man slammed down the phone and bounced up, smile at the ready.

"*Cette voiture, par là, le deux chevaux,*" I began, pointing out the door. "*Je suis curieuse . . .*" We advanced out the door.

"*Oui. Elle est à vendre,*" he said, anticipating my question.

My heart stopped. *Elle*—she—the feminine gender made us allies—was for sale. My brain was no longer operational.

I stood, momentarily transfixed. At close hand, the car looked to be in perfect condition, almost brand-new. Monsieur, who seemed to be very good at mind reading, said that it was in top condition, had very little mileage (approximately 11,000 km), and, in fact, was highly prized as the last of the *deux chevaux* models made.

I explained my situation: the house, my twice-yearly visits, the expenditure of rental cars, and my desire to buy a car of my own—and the concomitant problem of finding a place to keep the car.

He said he could keep the car. He had a second garage and always had extra space.

But this would mean I would need a way to and from the St-Denis train station.

He could pick me up. *Pas de problème.*

What had seemed insurmountable was suddenly easily being solved.

Was I interested?

I nodded, perhaps a little too vigorously. "*Oui!*"

He was *pressé* at the moment, he said, but if I'd like, I could drop by tomorrow at around noon and take a spin in the car. Indeed, he had a jumpy, mildly distracted air—which turned out to be characteristic—as if he had many other important matters on his mind. Despite this tiny village and modest business, he appeared to be an incredibly busy man.

I introduced myself. He didn't volunteer his name, as if this was an unnecessary, or perhaps too time-consuming bit of information to impart. I said that I would be back tomorrow. *À midi?*

D'accord.

I know I am a compulsive person. The delay would give me time to cool my fever and approach this with some degree of rationality.

Instead, it only heightened my delirium. I could think of nothing but the car. Actually, I know nothing about cars. As I live in New York, I am totally dependent on the subway. I don't know one car from another—a failing of my mother's that used to annoy me when I was growing up, when the acquisition of a driver's license, the use of the family car, and models of cars were of major significance. She seemed oblivious to all this. Yet here I was— around the age my mother was then—in the same state of ignorance. I knew that cars in the States cost a bundle. The asking price for the Citroën certainly didn't seem outrageous. It was possible; I would get a loan.

At noon I reappeared at the garage. The manager was once again on the phone, firing off clipped sentences like gunshots into the receiver. He hung up, stabbed his cigarette in an ashtray spilling over with butts, and delivered me an I'll-be-with-you-in-a-minute smile as he scribbled on a notepad. I meandered outside to moon over the *deux chevaux.*

Soon he bounded out of the garage. He opened the door on the driver's side for me and came around to sit in the passenger seat. The *deux chevaux* is a study in functionality of design. The dials are as plain as can be. The fat black knob of the gearshift is nearly the size of a tennis ball and fills a cupped hand. The passenger and driver windows are a hoot. They are divided in half horizontally. The lower flap is released with the flick of a catch; this section then swings outward and is cinched in place by another external catch. The motion required to open the window is like that of a hook shot in basketball. One has no choice about the degree of ventilation as with roll-up windows; it's open or shut, period. Another source of ventilation, and fog control, is the vent running along the dashboard, which can be regulated by the twist of a knob. The control of the miniature heating system is about the size of a cigarette pack, with a tiny knobbed latch that can be slipped into notches for low, medium, or high. That's about it—just the basics. The seats of this model were a soft dove gray—a rather plush look, I thought. It had a sunroof that would unsnap and roll up behind the backseat—for a sporty look, and, of course, the ultimate in ventilation.

The manager showed me the simple movement of the gear for reverse, first, second, third, and fourth. Off we went, down the road toward Vayrac. I was on top of the world, sailing along. There is a special feeling in driving the *deux chevaux*—or, I should say, it made *me* feel quite special. Majesterial: I felt I was riding high above the road. In command: the wheel, in comparison with compact American or European cars, is oversized; you can rest flare-elbowed on the rim. So authentic: the car is quintessentially French, indigenous. It would look ridiculous in any other country. Here it would look proper parked in front of a café or *pâtisserie*, in the drive of a château, alongside a country stream casting a shadow for a picnic. This particular *deux chevaux*, black and red, evoked Stendhal and dark passions. Yet the model was called Charleston, which had a nice, jazzy American ring.

It was a *coup de foudre*, love at first sight. I was incapable of objectivity. I didn't even consider shopping around (but then, I'm not one to shop around for a dress, either). And hadn't there been that prescient moment with Marilyn and Charles? I wondered if, in fact, the car I had seen with them was the exact same one. It was destiny.

We drove back to the garage. I stood beside the car, assuming a posture of deep thought and intense decision making. Of course, I should offer a lower price. You had to do that. The manager lit a cigarette. I heaved a sigh, meant as a sign of regret that I couldn't afford what he was proposing. After briefly haggling, he agreed to a slightly lower price. It could have been shaved a mere fraction from the asking price and I would have thought it a victory.

And how was I going to pay for the car? he wanted to know. I had no idea. I explained that I would have to go immediately to the BNP, in Biars-sur-Céré, where I have a bank account. The town was an approximate twenty-minute drive away. I forewarned him that I didn't have the francs at the moment, but I would see what could be worked out and I'd be back.

At the BNP, a small branch of the national bank, I explained the situation to the woman teller with whom I always have my dealings. Unlike my New York bank, with its battery of tellers behind bulletproof glass and bleeping neon-green lights to indicate the next available employee, she is only one of two tellers and has become a familiar welcoming face behind the counter. She has curly black hair and a gap between her two front teeth that she worries with her tongue when she counts bills in a rapid-fire blur.

"Superbe!" she remarked at my choice of automobile. But I would have to see the bank manager. Yes, he was here. *Une petite seconde.*

When the bank manager emerged from a side office, I felt a surge of confidence. He was not the stodgy old-timer who might resist the unorthodoxy of my request, but a stylish young man who said that he was delighted to make the acquaintance of one of their foreign clients. This seemed promising. He escorted me into his office and asked how he could assist me.

"J'ai trouvé la voiture de mes rêves!" I exploded. The car of my dreams was a black-and-red *deux chevaux*, I informed him. A 1990.

"Ah, une voiture collectionnée," he said, with some feeling.

I explained that the car was at the garage in Bétaille.

"Charron," he said noncommittally, referring to the owner.

I told him the price. He did not balk. Then I proposed my idea: that I borrow the money from the BNP and, upon my return to New York, take out a loan for the same amount from my bank and immediately repay the BNP.

How long might that take? he wondered, seemingly amenable. I paused, figuring. I was staying at my house for another week, I explained, before driving back to Paris. Once home, I guessed that it would take a week or so to get approval on a loan from my bank. But then I could make a direct transfer of funds from the New York BNP, which would expedite matters.

"Alors, un mois," he summed up, one month. He smiled broadly. He seemed to be enjoying the moment. Wouldn't it be nice to be a banker with the power to wave a magic wand and make dreams come true?

He reached for the phone; he would speak to Monsieur Jean-Paul Charron. I was dizzy with the rapidity of the transaction. And this was France, the land of endless red tape. In a suddenly commanding voice, he explained the arrangement to Charron, interrupted periodically when, I presumed, Charron was pummeling him with questions. The bank, he said, would issue Charron a check for the total amount, which he was to hold until the BNP received my check in return. Then, to my utter astonishment, he officiously yet gracefully informed Charron that I would need the use of the car during the remainder of my stay. And that I would be along shortly with the check. He hung up. Now, he said, I would need insurance on the car. Would I allow him to call his friend at the agency just down the road? I could stop there on my way back to Bétaille.

Check in hand, insurance in hand—we in the States have much to learn about customer service—I headed back to the garage.

I handed Monsieur Charron the check, unable to resist a slight flourish. Gone was the veneer of pleasantness. He was solemn and nervous—not without reason, perhaps—scrutinizing my driver's license as if it was an impenetrable puzzle or as if it might reveal a prison record. This, I'll admit, was somewhat understandable. Its mind-boggling string of numbers is daunting. He said, at last, that he would have the transaction papers for me to sign within two or three days. There was no mention of a charge for garaging the car or shepherding me back and forth from the train, and I didn't bring it up. See how it goes, I thought. Then—with a plastic smile—he handed me *les clefs*, the keys. I left him those to my rented car, which would remain at the garage until I picked it up to go back to Paris at the end of the week. Then, kiss rental cars good-bye forever!

I drove away in my new car, floating on a cloud of incredulity. I parked Charleston—as I'd decided to call her—at the house. Though there is the open garage, I resisted the steep uphill drive and chose a patch of lawn beside the stone wall leading to the house. After lunch, I washed and waxed the car. It glistened, from windshield wipers, which reminded me of slanted eyebrows, to hubcaps. I walked in admiring circles around it. That afternoon I puttered about the house, making periodic excursions to the front door to admire my car. I showed it off, of course, to the Bézamats (*"Ooh, elle est belle!"* said Madame. *"Pas de radio?"* Kati asked, incredulous) and the Hirondes (*"Une voiture collectionnée,"* said Raymond, echoing the bank manager, and tapping his forehead with an index finger to signal a clever move). During the week I made any excuse I could find to tool around: to St-Céré on shopping trips, to Rocamadour to look for a pair of candlesticks, to Cazillac for bread, to Meyssac for its *jour du marché*. Wherever I drove, I felt, whether real or imagined, the object of everyone's admiration. Every time I returned to the car, I inwardly beamed. *Elle est à moi!*

That weekend I was on the lookout for announcements of local festivals—anything to give me an excuse to take a spin with Charleston. Festivals are often announced with banners strung high across village streets. I spotted one for a cheese festival taking place in Rocamadour.

Tables were set up in an open field above the town for the *dégustation* of local cheeses and Cahors wine. I sampled the most wonderful Cantal, a mellow cheese of the neighboring *département* of the Auvergne, and bought a slab to bring home.

Most of the wines were from 1988 or 1989. I sampled a few from tiny plastic cups, enjoying the sunshine and the parade of families—with kids and dogs gamboling about—whiling away a Sunday afternoon. At one table, a farmer woman was offering homemade stuffed cabbage in small tin containers, perfect for one. That would be dinner, heated up.

When I got home, there was time for a long run. After a shower, I sat on the patio to read. But with the distraction of birdsong and the presence of Charleston, which I could glimpse out of the corner of my eye, the book rested idle in my lap. It was time to heat up the stuffed cabbage. How had the day slipped away?

Early Tuesday morning, I closed the house, dropped the keys with the Bézamats, and returned to the garage for the swap of cars with Monsieur Charron. I explained that I would be back in late October and would write him well in advance to notify him of the exact day and train. *Au revoir!*

The rental car felt low on the road, lightweight, dull. I was instantly reduced to a mundane American-with-the-rental-car status. That evening I had planned a splurge for the finale of my trip, an overnight stay at the château de Vault-de-Lugny, in Burgundy, on my circuitous way back to Paris. I'd read about the château in one of my French newsletters, which are highly reliable sources for hotels and restaurants in both Paris and the country. It had waxed lyrical about the château, calling it "one of

the most unique places we have ever visited in the world
. . . a dream château in every respect."

The drive took seven hours. I pulled up to the towering
wrought-iron gate, which was shut. I got out of the car
and rang the bell. A small voicebox statically greeted me:
bonjour, with a question mark. I announced myself and
the gates slowly began to open. I jumped back into the
car and drove slowly through the gates, which opened to
an enchanted world. The drive to the château circled
around a perfectly trimmed lush green lawn with flowers
in a riot of color. Ducks and geese—and a peacock!—
strolled lazily about.

This had been a fortified château; its stone turrets,
crenellated guard towers, and moat still attested to its
historic past. Burgundian architecture was reflected in
its tall sixteenth-century watchtower, the seventeenth-
century house, and rambling eighteenth- and nineteenth-
century farm buildings. I'd read in the newsletter that
today it is a family home run by a Monsieur Matherat-
Audan and his daughter, Elisabeth. It was the latter, a
beautiful and totally unaffected young woman, who
greeted me at the reception desk, located in the entrance
hall of the château. It was appointed with antiques, but
still cozy. I admired a breakfront that contained bibelots
and, surprisingly, a collection of three tiny birds' nests.

My room, also furnished with antiques, overlooked the
idyllic lawn scene. I threw open the long French windows. There was time before dinner to stretch my legs after the drive. I wandered off through the woods on the
grounds of the château, following a gurgling stream.
Immediately I was joined—or, I should say, herded
along—by a great golden dog. Deeper into the woods, I
came upon a horse idly munching on some grass by the

stream. I petted his soft red mane and velvety snout. This was a world one usually sees only in children's books.

After a long bubble bath, I sat in a wrought-iron chair on the lawn with a champagne aperitif before dinner. The sun was casting a rosy light and there was now a slight chill in the air. A jet-black Labrador retriever curled up by my chair, his head propped on my shoe. "Licorice! Licorice!" I heard a woman's singsong voice beckoning the dog distantly from the château. Just the barest flicker of an ear. Her ineffectual calls died away. Feeling pampered and blissful, I went in to dinner, which was served at a great wooden table, *tâble d'hôte* style, in the first-floor kitchen.

In the morning I was up at seven-thirty for a run. Luckily, a young maid was walking along the drive to open the front gate for me. Suddenly Licorice was at my heels. All along the way, he darted ahead or lagged behind, as one thing or another caught his attention—including a flock of sheep, who bolted at his approach like tall grasses whipped by the wind. In the last stretch back to the château, he ran at an even pace alongside me—the first time I'd ever run with a dog.

After breakfast, I stopped at the front desk to check out with Elisabeth and told her that the château had been one of my favorite places in all of France (another place I vowed to return to). She glowed. After paying the bill, I paused. I'd been thinking about those birds' nests.

"*J'ai une question. . . .*" I began hesitantly. I pointed to the nests in the breakfront. Elisabeth rose and came around the desk. We stood side by side, peering through the glass to admire their remarkable construction. Then I said that what I was about to ask would probably seem bizarre. She looked expectant. Could I buy one?

She laughed in startled amazement. No, she wouldn't sell me one, she said emphatically, but she would *give* me one, of course, "if that's your pleasure," she added in English. Then, like a child about to reveal a secret, she drew me outside the front door. At one side, there was a small tree no taller than myself. *"Regardez,"* she said, pointing to it. I saw nothing remarkable. She led me closer and pointed again. *"Regardez,"* she repeated in a low whisper. And then I saw a tiny yellow bird, perhaps a finch, sitting on her little nest. We watched in silence for several minutes as she twitched her head and flitted about the nest, like a windup toy, and then Elizabeth drew me away. She explained that this bird builds her nest in that same spot every year, so that the nest I chose would be replaced.

She wrapped my nest gingerly in a double layer of tissue paper. It was so tiny that it would fit in the palm of my hand. Never have I carried something so ephemeral and delicate: it weighed no more than, well, a feather. After I got home, I started looking for some sort of container to protect it from my curious cats. One weekend, at an antiques shop in the country, I discovered a tiny wire basket with a latched lid, used for carrying eggs. The nest fit perfectly inside, but was still visible from without. An *objet d'art*. Every so often I ponder its intricacy. It has bits of down and feather still clinging to it, vestiges of that sweet bird, a remembrance of that French haven.

12

A NEW GARAGE

About a month before my trip in the fall, I wrote Monsieur Charron that I would be arriving on the two fifty-three train in St-Denis on October 19. The plane from New York, however, was delayed two hours, so that I missed both the nine thirty-three and ten o'clock trains from Paris to Brive—a trip of approximately four hours—where I was to connect up with the tiny train to St-Denis, another half-hour journey. Now, as it was, I wouldn't get into St-Denis until six thirty-six, just when I wanted this first arrangement with Charron to go smoothly. I phoned the garage from Paris and, when he wasn't there, left the message with the young woman who answered the phone.

I slept on the train—jet lag taking its toll. When I arrived in St-Denis, Monsieur Charron was standing on the platform, and not looking especially delighted to see me. I was all apologies. He shrugged, implying at least that it wasn't my fault. On the ride back to the garage, he was formal and unforthcoming. Perhaps he was resenting, after all, the role of chauffeur—he certainly wasn't the type—or perhaps he was merely annoyed at the inconvenience of the delay.

Or perhaps he was feeling the object of suspicion. Marilyn and Charles had been to the house in July, when Monsieur Bézamat informed them that Charron was freely driving the car all around—he'd spotted him as far as Brive. My arrangement with Monsieur Charron had been that he would move the car from time to time, say from one of his garages to the other, just to keep the engine tuned up. I had informed the insurance company of this. My policy covered the car only during my visits (I only had to inform the agency when I arrived and departed).

Marilyn and Charles had stopped by the garage, introduced themselves, and on the pretext of interest in my new car, said they wanted to look it over. Charles then surreptitiously checked the mileage: 13,502. When I purchased the car, the mileage had been approximately 11,000, and I estimated that I couldn't have put more than 1,000 kilometers on the car when I was there. (Monsieur Charron had, indeed, been more than tuning up the car.)

It was dark. I was hungry and tired. I thanked Monsieur Charron kindly—I wasn't going to bring up the indelicate matter until I had more information from Monsieur Bézamat—and jumped into Charleston. *Belle voiture!* Now the meter read precisely 13,502, I noted. Could Marilyn and Charles have aroused his suspicion, so that he stopped his gallivanting? I drove to the Bézamats for the keys. We gathered around the table.

Monsieur Bézamat, shutting his eyes and tapping me on the shoulder in a conspiratorial way, confided that, yes, he'd seen Charron driving all around. Big shrug of shoulders, as if to say, "What did you expect?"

"*C'est à sa copine,*" Kati chimed in, with a knowing air. His girlfriend's car! So. "*Sa copeeen,*" I shrieked. That explained a lot.

"*Allez à Hironde,*" Monsieur Bézamat advised. "*Il a sa grange.*" The barn. Perfect.

It was so cold and dark that I decided not to open the house that night. I drove into the village for dinner and an overnight stay at the Vieux Quercy. After a restorative hot bath, I settled into the cheery, brightly lit dining room with a kir. A young woman seated with three other people approached my table. She held out my wallet. This must be yours, she said. You're American, yes? They had found it in the parking lot on their way into dinner. My heart flipped! After Monsieur Charron's duplicity, my faith was renewed.

The Vieux Quercy is a bargain. My dinner included an appetizer of *escargots,* a *confit* with a light citron sauce and potatoes, a selection of cheeses, and dessert and coffee. Over dinner, I briefly considered the situation with Charron. I'd thought of confronting him with the facts of the mileage, the insurance policy, and so forth. But now I was convinced after seeing the Bézamats that I'd have to make another arrangement. Raymond's barn could be the solution, but it would be asking a lot of him.

I'd planned to spend several days in the Auvergne (*Les Logis* in hand) and dropped in on the Hirondes early in the morning before I left. Simone was back from a thermal cure in the Pyrenees. She was bereft, she said, her eyes welling. Her sister, who lived in Paris, and her sister-in-law, who lived in Brive, had both died recently, within weeks of each other. Her face was drained, her voice dispirited. She was locked up in grief, isolated in her sorrow. She shuddered in an attempt to shake off her mood in my presence.

Raymond appeared, his hair damp and slicked as if he'd just showered, fumbling with a shirt button as if he'd just finished dressing. After greeting me, he peeked out the window. *"Le Charleston,"* he said approvingly. Where did I keep it? he wanted to know.

This gave me my opening. Yet I was uncertain if Raymond and Charron might not have some association of which I was unaware. I attempted to explain the problem diplomatically: perhaps this was Monsieur Charron's idea of keeping the car tuned up, perhaps he didn't understand the insurance business, etc. But I was in a quandary as to what to do.

Raymond snorted. No question now of where we stood. Without another moment's hesitation, he offered to keep the car. He had all that space in the barn, where the car would be safe and protected. Of course he could drive me to and from the train. The plan had unfolded so naturally that I didn't feel I was being a burden. Raymond, in fact, seemed rather tickled at the idea.

Charleston performed stalwartly in the rugged terrain of the Auvergne, one of the least populated *départements* of France. The area doesn't see many tourists, and at this time of year it was especially desolate—thus, especially appealing to me. I felt I'd penetrated the back roads, the depths of France. The red-tile roofs and creamy stonework of the houses in the Lot gave way to gray slate and white stucco. Tucked in small clusters, they blended perfectly with the gray moutain vistas dusted with snow. The

Hotel d'Entraigues, in Égliseneuve d'Entraigues, was a plain, no-frills *logis*. My room had a jarring decor of yellow-orange flowery wallpaper, a black-and-white linoleum floor with a motif of wormlike squiggles, and a red plastic chair. It was unintended kitsch.

I took a long walk after the long drive. There were mahogany cows and breathtaking mountain views. A light snow began to fall, etching the pine trees. In only a matter of hours, I was a world away from Pech Farguet. When I got back to the inn, I learned that the *salle de bain* was down the hall and was available for a small fee. I lay back in the ancient, enormous—that is to say, human-length—tub, feeling puffed up with the steam. I could have fallen asleep, but my stomach was calling out for nourishment.

The only other customers in the dining room were a cheery British couple, complete with entertaining English chatter. There was no menu; dinner consisted of a thick vegetable soup (similar to Madame Bézamat's), roast veal with a mountain of rice, and a bowl of lettuce dressed with a rich vinaigrette dressing. Madame left the cheese board on the table, so I was free to have as much as I wanted: Cantal *doux*, St-Nectaire, and *bleu*. Dessert offered a wide choice of ice cream. I chose *myrtille*—blueberry—and vanilla. The last was the best vanilla ice cream—the true test of ice cream—I'd ever had, pale yellow from the egg-yolk enrichment and speckled with vanilla-bean seeds. I ordered a second dish! A second helping is hardly ever as good as the first; even a second bite is not as good as the first. This, however, was.

After a few brutally cold days, I left the winter climate behind, circling back through the town of Aurillac. In the old quarter, now a pedestrian shopping center, there's a wonderful old-world cheese shop, the Cremière Leroux, which glistens with white tiles and marble. Enormous wheels of Cantal sit on the counter, with a choice of either aged or sweet, the younger type. Raymond had told me he prefers the sweet, so I bought some of this for him and the aged variety for me.

I came back to late fall in the Lot. Mornings in the valley were laden with fog; from my perch in the house, it lay like a cloudy carpet at my feet. If I drove into St-Céré for my coffee, I had to turn on the headlights—but by noon the sun would break through so that the earth warmed and the trees glistened from the dew.

I wanted to sever the Charron connection immediately and stopped by the garage as soon as I was back to explain politely that I'd worked out a more sensible arrangement with a neighbor. He gave me his rehearsed smile, and that was that. In Biars, I had the mud-caked car washed. I bought a Dustbuster and cleaned the interior. I bought a car cover for the wintering-over. Charleston sparkled! She was ready for hibernation.

For the trip back to Paris, I planned to catch the nine-fourteen morning train in St-Denis. Raymond advised me to get to the house by eight-thirty. It was a damp, chilly morning with a steady drizzle—to my consternation, since I'd just given Charleston a last polishing the evening before. When I arrived at the Hirondes, Raymond was stationed at the barn, which is just beside the house. With a deadly seriousness, like a *gendarme* directing traffic at the Place de la Concorde, he guided me inch by inch into the barn. He had laid down heavy sheets of cardboard to the right and rear of the barn, where Charleston would sit. I finally positioned the car to his satisfaction and deboarded with my single bag. He cursed the rain and explained that he wouldn't cover the car until she was thoroughly dry. He also reassured me that she would be absolutely safe. If he and Simone went away, the garage would be locked. And when they were home, he would park his car behind her so that a thief would have to steal his car first!

We went to the house for a coffee. Simone wanted to show me something *extraordinaire*. She led me into the kitchen. There on the counter was an oversized *cèpe* with another, smaller one growing from the cap, piggyback-style. A woman friend, she said, had found it yesterday in the woods and Simone had said that she must show it to Madame Barry. This was no small thing to me: so, I held a place in her world beyond this room, this moment.

Simone was dressed as if for Sunday, in a green wool dress with a string of white beads. She and a friend had appointments at the hairdresser's and would be going with us as far as Bétaille. When we left the house, her woman friend was waiting by the car. Simone and her friend insisted on sitting in the back. We piled in. On the way, my journey back to the States was discussed in detail: the hours by train, by plane, in both directions. Simone's friend was astonished at the length of the air flight. Raymond, who collects and enjoys statistics of any kind, explained to her that the tailwinds made the trip from the States much shorter than the return.

We dropped the women off by the bakery; they each unfolded a little plastic rain cap over their head, despite the fact that they were minutes from the hairdresser. On we went.

We were at the station shortly after nine. The station is the hub of St-Denis—if that's the word for a dull and generally lifeless outpost. (The town's very name, St-Denis-

Près-Martel, connotes its decidedly kid-sister status.) I told Raymond that he needn't wait with me for the train, but he insisted. He likes to watch the trains, he said. As we stood on the platform he explained, with an obvious pride, that his son worked for the SNCF, the French railroad. According to French law, this allowed Raymond, as his father (though not Simone, who was not his birth mother) free, unlimited travel, so oftentimes he took short excursions by himself on the weekends. His son's children, he added, could ride at half price until age eighteen.

The shrill whistle of the little train was heard in the distance. I thanked Raymond for the favor of taking the car and driving me to the station. As I shook his hand I slipped a hundred-franc bill into his palm. He waved it back at me, but I planted my hands behind my back. I'm confident I read him correctly: he was grateful.

I love a train. Traveling by rail gives you a sense of real time, a spirit of adventure, drama, and the possibility of romance (although the rhythmic clack of wheels on track, the cradle sway, usually puts me to sleep). The train pulling into the St-Denis station was nearly stagecoach size. Passengers gazed from the windows of its two cars, some in boredom, some in mild curiosity. It came to a trembling stop. Raymond gave me a hand up as I mounted the high step. I sat down at the station-side window. He was still standing on the platform and gave me a gentle wave. I waved back. *"Au revoir,"* I mouthed. There was a sudden ache in my chest. Raymond's figure blurred into an image of my father, who, when I'd last seen him conscious, was standing on a train platform waving farewell as I departed for Europe. The train started up with a small jolt. I glanced back. Raymond was watching the train move out, his arm raised, seemingly forgotten, in midair.

13

ON THE ROAD

In the spring of 1993, when my office closed for a week, I tagged on my two-week vacation. With the luxury of three weeks, I could make a long pilgrimage, albeit solely for pleasure, with Charleston. I decided on Provence, the region most people dream of when they think of the French countryside. I hadn't been back since Jean and I were there years before. Then we had had the fortune of staying in the summerhouse owned by a Parisian couple who were Jean's friends, which was located on a hilltop in Cagna-sur-Mer outside Nice. This trip I aimed to explore the less glittery side of the region, going the *logis* route.

France is the land of pilgrimages, and I have always been fascinated by their history. Before I left for France, I resurrected my *Canterbury Tales.*

> *Whan that April with his showres soote*
> *The droughte of Marche hath perced to the roote,*

And bathed every veyne in swich licour,
Of which vertu engendred is the flowr;
When Zephyrus eek with his sweete breeth
Inspired hath in every holt and heeth
The tendre croppes, and the yonge sonne
Hath in the Ram his halve cours yronne,
And smale fowles maken melodye
That sleepen al the night with open yë—
So priketh hem Nature in hir corages—
Thanne longen folk to goon on pilgrimages. . . .

When I read that last line, I was confused: I thought a pilgrimage was supposed to be a penitential exercise or an attempt to seek a cure for oneself or a relative. Or, on the lowest scale, a sentence for committing a civil offense, something like our system of community service in lieu of incarceration—and who would be longing to share the road with robbers, rapists, and murderers?

I talked over the subject with Charles, who shed more light on the matter. In the eleventh century, he said, the practice of going on pilgrimages satisfied a deep need among adventurous, perhaps marginally literate, and pious folk. Christians venerated relics and believed that cures of body and soul could be achieved by arduous journeys to shrines where the remains of holy persons were kept. The growing number of monasteries fostered this trend, providing way stations where pilgrims could eat and sleep (and spend money). Competition between monasteries to attract pilgrims grew intense. Some pilgrimages, like that to St. James of Campostela in Northwestern Spain, became immensely popular and safer alternatives to the risky voyage to the Holy Land. The popular conception of pilgrimages is that they were undertaken in order to atone for some grave sin. Actually, although some of the harsher or more spectacular pilgrimages might have been performed as penance, the great majority seem to have been a mixture of personal devotion, fulfilling adventure, wanderlust, or mercantile opportunity. Sharing experiences, risks, and hardships must have built that same sense of solidarity, mutual confidence, fellow feeling, and occasional hilarity that twentieth-century man feels during a long bus ride or after a scary airplane landing.

Most people who lived between the fourth and the fifteenth centuries never went more than a day's walk away from their birthplace. To be a pilgrim one had to be able to leave behind occupation, home, and loved ones (pilgrims rarely traveled with their families). Peasants, farmers, serfs, and slaves, who weren't free to leave, were unlikely to go on pilgrimage. More pilgrims came from among the single folk (young widows and widowers were much more common then), and from among town or city dwellers. They had heard travelers' tales, and were itching to go themselves. Most pilgrims only went once in their lives, but eighteen months is a big chunk out of a life expectancy of thirty-five years. Wealthier pilgrims traveled in comfort; these could afford better food, horses or mules, and servants. Many others started and returned nearly penniless, depending on charity throughout their trip.

Pilgrimages took many months and often years. You traveled light, with a bedroll, a staff, and a cloak. A scallop shell that pinned up the brim of your floppy felt hat told everyone you met that you were a pilgrim on the way to Campostela. Even today, the French call scallops the shells of St. James (*coquilles St-Jacques*). Pilgrims traveled singly or in bands of varying sizes. This depended on how safe they felt the countryside was, whether they could keep up with the party, and whether they felt comfortable with each other. All across Southwestern France there are braided routes that the pilgrims followed from minor shrine to major site, all ending in a crossing of the Pyrenees into Spain.

My pilgrimage to Provence was undertaken in unabashed wanderlust. I had only one slight upset with Charleston. It was in Avignon, which I found difficult to negotiate by car. I circled and circled and found nowhere to park on the street. At a sign for the Palais des Papes— the principal focus of my visit—I turned and found myself irrevocably committed to a dark underground garage. I resist underground garages at all costs. I fear I'll lose track of the location of my car, that I'll become trapped in a mechanized system I don't comprehend. I am a person who balks at an automatic stamp machine—even one with instructions in English. But there was no retreat. I parked on a level where there was plenty of space and took my ticket from the automatic dispenser. CAISSE 3, the sign read. I emblazoned it on my mind. I rode the *ascenseur* with a British couple, who seemed equally at sea—"Darling, you will remember which ramp?" We were belched out of the elevator into a prisonlike concrete passageway that eventually led to a street behind the *palais*.

In the center of its courtyard was a gargantuan Botero sculpture of a nude astride a bull, a hilarious affront to its venue. The entire building had been turned over to an extensive Botero exhibition—to the horror of a tour group of proper British ladies in summer frocks and flowery straw hats, who found it "shocking" and "disgusting." I wandered through the great halls until lunchtime, delighted that I'd stumbled on the irreligious Botero show. Then I took my carefully memorized circuitous route back to the *ascenseur*, congratulating myself when I found Caisse 3 and Charleston without difficulty. At the end of the spiraling ramp, I handed my ticket through the window to the man in the booth.

"*Vous n'avez pas payé?*" he demanded, in a disapproving manner.

But where was I to have paid?

"*Non,*" I replied, the claustrophobic heat of the garage mounting.

"*Descendez,*" he said in a tone used for children. This was a man who would exercise his authority to the hilt. He motioned to a machine on the opposite side of a concrete embankment.

Two cars were now backed up behind me. I jumped from the car and followed him. He inserted my ticket into a slot in the machine and pointed to the fee registered. I fumbled through the change in my wallet and came up with an inexact amount. In aggravating slow motion, he took the coins from my sweating palm and dropped them in. The change rattled into the cup. I scooped it up and raced back to the car. There was not a honk from the patient line of cars, probably tourists like myself, dreading a similar humiliation. I drove out of the garage into the welcome light of day, my distrust in garage parking confirmed.

Few places—the restaurant, the inn—remain fixed in my memory as time passes: I have to go to diaries to summon them up again. Les Hospitaliers, in Le Poët-Laval, which I'd read about in Pat Wells's *Food Lover's Guide to France* and which was a splurge, is one that will remain ineradicable. It encapsulates that Provence trip. The hotel's architecture merged with the crumbling white stone-work that was the last vestige of this remote medieval mountain hamlet. The village was a Pompeii, with the hotel a phoenix rising from its ruin. This was the first place I'd ever visited in France where I literally could not go for a run—the road down was a sheer drop to the valley. There was a pool, sprinkled with flower petals from the surrounding trees, which I had to myself for a swim before dinner. My room overlooked the terrace, where a fir tree right out of a Van Gogh painting stood like a tall spear against the sky and morning glories spilled over hedges.

To get to the separate restaurant, I had to climb up a steep rocky terrace to a great wooden door. It creaked as it opened onto a spectacular setting. The restaurant of creamy-white stone was semi-alfresco, with a view of the surrounding hills, hazy in the evening light. Flowers and candles adorned the tables. It was as serene as a monastery.

I ordered a glass of champagne and chose the *prix fixe* menu. Here, as the view of the hills darkened, is what I had: the chef's offering of an *amuse-gueule* (what we would call a cocktail snack but which wittily translates as "tease the mouth," and specifically, the mouth of a ravenous animal), which was a puff of *pâté à chou* filled with *crème fraîche* atop a delicate chive cream sauce; an eggplant mousse in an airy cream sauce with a refreshing touch of mint; a salad of finely slivered avocado on delicate mixed greens, with olives and mounds of avocado mousse; for the main course, what was called a *crespinet du pied de porc*, molded balls of rich, gamy minced pork in a crisp casing, sweet and sticky, surrounded by tiny carmelized onions, bacon bits, and baby carrots; an unusual cheese course, a *chèvre rôti* redolent of anise and warming its bed of greens; and, finally, a *reine de pommes*, a warm slab of apple tart in a cidery sauce. I spent more on the wine than the entire meal: a 1985 Graves recommended by the wine steward, who enacted the classic and mesmerizing ritual—which I've so rarely seen—of testing the wine in a little silver cup (called a *taste-vin*) and holding the bottle to candlelight to check the sediment. It was a grand wine; at the end, he pointed to the sediment on the side of the bottle—a good sign. I received every bit as much solicitous attention as the elegant couple, apparently known to the maître d', seated at the next table. I walked back to my room—no stars, portending a cloudy day—literally and figuratively on top of the world.

Rosebushes lined the wine route. At first I assumed they simply reflected the Provençals' love of flowers. But I later read that since roses are easily susceptible to rot, they warn viticulturists of impending disease to their vines. The fields were carpeted with *genêts*, buttercup-yellow wildflowers with a powerful perfume. With the windows of Charleston open, and the ceaseless *mistral* sending rushes of air through the car, I was constantly inhaling the aroma. I took to stopping along the way to pick a few sprays of *genêts*, which I'd stick in a water glass in my hotel room, their scent my last sensation before sleep. The rolling yellow fields, the deep blue sky, brought Monet's blue-and-yellow kitchen at Giverny to mind.

Along the Cézanne route outside of Aix, to Mont-St-Victoire, the colors of the landscape became muted, austere. My art-history books came to life, and I recognized the places where Cézanne's strivings to find "a harmony parallel to nature" were realized. I drove the route around the rugged limestone massif and circled back to Le Tholonet, where Cézanne had rented an old stone farmhouse in the last years of his life. Being within sight of St-Victoire, the circumstances of his death seemed particularly poignant: he'd gone out on one of his daily excursions to paint the mountain and was caught in a rainstorm. Burdened with his easel, he collapsed on the road and was eventually found by someone with a laundry cart. He died a week later.

The *mistral* was maddening, a never-ending brewing storm. How do the Provençals endure this wind day in, day out? What would the winters be like? I asked Madame, as she anchored my tablecloth at an alfresco lunch; her smile and shrug seemed to say, "We all have our little crosses, but this is a small one to pay for being in paradise." But after two weeks, I was itching to be free of it. The last day, as I headed back to Pech Farguet, I wondered at what point the *mistral* would vanish—would there be one instance when it was and the next instant not? I couldn't say when—it was like waiting for a flower to bloom, or die—but at some point the car was no longer buffeted, the whistling stilled, and when I stepped out the door, it was as if the world had come to rest. Provence was behind me.

Crossing the border of the Lot, I marveled again at the singular character of the region: the old stone houses with red-tiled roofs, the gentle landscape, the colors. The very air, it seemed, was unlike any other. I took a deep breath and drank it in. In all of France, I was reassured yet again, this was exactly where I wanted to be.

14

AN OLD FRIEND

The following fall, my close friend Patsy O'Connell visited the house. Our friendship has been long and loyal. We grew up in adjacent neighborhoods and had gone to school together, all the way from first grade through college. We both had reclusive, pessimistic Irish fathers. I don't recall our ever speaking of them to each other. Our mothers were Brownie leaders together. They were the center of our lives. We both had two much older siblings, sisters in Patsy's case, brothers in mine, so that we shared the experience of having older parents and a more solitary upbringing. Only in her later years did Patsy become spontaneously generous—a streak of Irish miserliness of spirit overcome? Yet she is still somewhat shy about demonstrating—and receiving—physical affection. We formed a bond in those early years that underwent dramatic changes in our lives. During college, we segued into antithetical circles. Patsy got involved with a radical antiestablishment hippie crowd (she was arrested

in one of the first sit-down protests against racial prej-
udice in a bank in St. Louis). I took a staid path: so-
rority, religious sodality, honors society (the be-good,
don't-rock-the-boat route). Yet we remained close friends.
Our contrary worlds were almost an unspoken joke between us.

Patsy joined the Peace Corps and subsequently taught
in Africa for several years. Eventually she wound up back
in St. Louis—the majority of her close friends were
there—as the director of an adult-education program. She
recently bought a three-story house in the historic reno-
vated district of Souillard, near the waterfront, which she
has filled with her collection of African art and a colorful
array of folk art. Her married sister lives in New Jersey,
however, and Patsy usually visits her once a year and
stays over for a night in Brooklyn; I get back to St. Louis
now and then to see her and other friends. Even though
we're far apart, I count her as one of my closest friends.
And though we see each other infrequently, there's a continuity. I couldn't stand on more solid ground than with
this woman I've known all my life. I invited her to
France, assured that we'd travel well together: same interests, same rhythm. And we'd worn well.

Being in France together would be special, since we'd
have an extended period of time—five days—all to ourselves. I arrived several days early, on a Friday, and
planned to pick up Patsy at the train station in Brive the
following Monday (to save her the anxiety of having to
switch trains to St-Denis).

When I drove up to the station she was already standing on the steps. We hugged gleefully. Here we were, two
old grade-school friends meeting in Brive! On the way
out of town, we chattered madly, about Paris, her train
ride, about the weather, about the route we'd be taking

home. She adored Charleston. Such a *typique* way to get about! She was rhapsodic along the route to the house. Not far from Brive, there's a particularly spectacular view of the château of Turenne, with the houses of the tiny village clustered at its base like children at their mother's skirt (in fact, it had more than a thousand villages and numerous abbeys under its aegis). It was her first castle and I slowed to a crawl so that she could observe it at length.

At the house, she dropped her luggage on the patio, stunned at the view. I basked in the moment: Patsy at my home in France at last. We'd been planning this trip for a long while.

That evening we had champagne before the fire. I'd put together a special dinner: a potato *gratin* (a James Villas recipe that required about three hours of tending) and grilled duck breast in a port-and-orange sauce. We shared a bottle of wine and dropped happily in bed. Patsy had the upper bedroom. I slept in one of the two enormous chairs before the hearth, which had been built by Mr. Pinckney. These are capacious wooden chairs, with sturdy bright blue cushions (the color scheme of my house is a Monet-like blue and yellow, the same as Patsy's old bedroom at home, I remembered). They have sloping backs, and long footrests that slide out from the bottom so that you can almost stretch out full-length. It's somewhat like sleeping in a lounge chair. It was no sacrifice to be lulled to sleep by the dying embers of the fire.

Patsy reflects her Irish heritage. She is plump and apple-cheeked, with large blue-green eyes and curly auburn hair, which she now dyes. She is wonderfully witty and talks a mile a minute; when she and her sister are together they carry on an overlapping dialogue, speaking and hearing at the same time. Patsy loves nothing more than a lively and nearly endless discussion. She has a big, cackling laugh, which erupts often. When she is pensive, she has a winsome way of pursing her lips as if to kiss. Patsy enjoys good food, which gave me no end of pleasure during her stay. Each morning I would drive down to the Bétaille bakery while she was showering. After the first morning, she always wanted both a croissant and a *pain aux raisins*, with coffee. She clucked over the food like a contented hen.

I wanted to wow Patsy right off the bat. So, the first morning, we headed for Rocamadour, one of the most spectacular sights in the region. The village, seemingly defying gravity, is literally pinned to the face of a cliff over a gorge 1,640 feet below. Rocamadour was a major pilgrimage stop: according to the Michelin, thirty thousand people came on days of major pardon and plenary indulgence. Its fame grew as a result of miracles rewarding the faithful. On the way to Rocamadour, I told Patsy about the pilgrims' route, just as Charles had told me, in storybook fashion.

The arriving pilgrims, I said, entered the Haut-Quercy from the north. Perhaps a night or two in Tulle, and the hospitality of the abbot-bishop, would have whetted their desire to reach the shrine of the Black Virgin in Rocamadour. They would look forward to seeing Roland's sword, and to hearing the blessed bell that rang to mark the saving of sailors in trouble on the sea, far to the west. A day's walk would bring the ragged band to Aubazine, where, at the shrine of Blessed Stephen, they could receive blessings. Then they went south to the high castle of Turenne, where one of the most independent and powerful of French viscounts ruled, or perhaps by way of

Collonges-la-Rouge, where amid orchards and vines, rich farmers made the land glow like the finest of medieval miniatures. The pilgrims would come to the towers of Curemonte or Martel, tiny fortified cities, each with active markets and ruled by a dozen noble families. Then down to the cliff-bound valley of the swift-flowing Dordogne, crossing at Carennac, or farther west at Gluges. On the way the pilgrims passed farmers driving plows pulled by teams of four oxen. They met up with monks hurrying from priory to monastery to grange. They occasionally saw knights or men-at-arms, but these violent folk were best avoided. There were no bridges on the Dordogne, which was uncrossable when it flooded, and the ferryman's charge was probably very dear.

After resting on the south side of the river, the pilgrims would climb up to the plateau, the Causse of Gramat. The *causse* is a drier woodsy-bushy wilderness dotted here and there with sinkholes or depressions where a farmer can eke out a living. Shepherds pastured huge numbers of sheep on the *causse* in the Middle Ages, and orders like the Knights Templar owned huge expanses of its harsher and less populous parts. In summer the *causse* becomes fiercely hot, at least in comparison with the sweeter valleys to the north, and in winter the wind blows very cold. There is no surface water on the *causse*, and it is a very long day's walk across it to the edges of the deep canyon of the Alzou, which hides the wonderful shrine of Rocamadour.

The reward for those who reached l'Hospitalet, a village at the edge of the canyon, was a spectacular view of Rocamadour, with its buildings that seemed to pour down the cliff face to the west. Here the pilgrim could rest, find food and shelter, and prepare for days of devotion, sightseeing, and shopping. The first meal at l'Hospitalet would surely include slices of a huge round peasant loaf, the tasty disks of *cabecou* or goat cheese, and wine from the vineyards of Cahors. In the days that followed, the pilgrims would walk down the cliff road and through the fortified gate. They would pass dozens of small stalls, inns of every variety, and religious shrines for every type of devotion. Poor and rich alike, men as well as women, must all have felt the keen sense of satisfaction that a long effort to reach a distant goal brings. But pilgrimages are addictive, and how many of them would decide in a few days or weeks to continue on, to Conques or to St. James of Campostela in faraway Spain? After all, it would only take three or four more months to get there. The life of a pilgrim was both harsh and sweet, trudging, staff in hand, to new countryside, and a new blessing with every shrine. It's easy to see how the way of the pilgrim became one of the most powerful metaphors for the journey of human life.

The route to Rocamadour from my house has the best approach. The road winds through a tunnel and brings you out on the far side of the valley—*swoosh!*—just opposite the cliff and the suspended village. It takes your breath away. It did Patsy's.

At the far end of the village is a long (two hundred and twenty-three steps), steep staircase, with a plaque listing various notables that have climbed its taxing passage, ending with Raymond Jolle Fénelon, whose relationship to François of Carennac I am uncertain of. It reads, at the end, SUIVIS DE FOULES IMMENSE, ONT GRAVI CET ESCALIER À GÉNOUX (followed by enormous crowds, who have climbed this staircase on their knees). The stairway leads to a chapel at the summit, which houses the Black Virgin.

A penitent, having climbed the steps on *his* knees, with perhaps chains around his arms and neck, would present himself for purification before the statue. Patsy and I took the *ascenseur.*

Today, the tiny chapel is a grimy black, as if it suffered a devastating conflagration, though it's probably only centuries of accumulated candle soot. Two angels opposite the altar appear instead to be heralds from hell. My American eyes say this cries out for restoration, yet it certainly has an atmosphere to suit the Black Virgin. Patsy and I agreed that this statue has to be the ugliest in all of Christendom. She is perhaps two feet tall, seated with the Christ child on one knee; her crown, studded with what look like some cheap semiprecious stones, seems too heavy for her diminutive size. The two figures are blandly featureless. And strangely, sinfully black. Paradoxically, however, her peculiar size and forbidding color give her a certain poignancy and presence.

Outside the chapel is a recess in the stone wall, which reads: *ICI FUT DÉCOUVERT EN 1166 LE CORPS PARFAITEMENT CONSERVÉ DE ST. AMADOUR.* According to the Michelin, the identity of St. Amadour is a bit sketchy. The most accepted theory is that the perfectly preserved body belonged to Zaccheus, the husband of St. Veronica, who wiped the face of Christ on His way to Calvary. I hadn't known that St. Veronica was married, nor the rest of this story. They were obliged to flee Palestine and, guided by an angel, found their way to the Limousin. After Veronica died, Zaccheus took to preaching in the area.

How do we get from the name of Zaccheus to St. Amadour? Patsy wanted to know. The Michelin, at this point, requires a giant leap of faith. In its rather stunted translation of the French Michelin, it states: "It is pure legend but one thing is certain; there was a hermit and he knew the rock well as is [sic] often sheltered him. The *Langue d'Oc* expression—*roc amator*—he who likes the rock—established the name of this village sanctuary, which became Roc Amadour and finally Rocamadour."

We descended to the village, had a light lunch, and headed back to the car. As we approached the ramparts I saw that Charleston was obscured by an enormous tourist bus, devoid of passengers and driver. When we got closer, the full impossibility of our situation became apparent: the car was completely cornered, with not an inch to maneuver. We looked at each other and moaned.

Across the road, near the souvenir shop, a group of men were hanging out, conversing and smoking as if they had nothing better to do. These had to be the bus drivers. I approached one and explained my dilemma. Ah, he tsked, I had parked in a space reserved for the buses. The tour group wouldn't be returning until four o'clock, maybe four-thirty. It was now two o'clock. No, he shook his head at my plea, the bus couldn't be moved. To do so would require moving the other bus alongside. And that driver wasn't even around, probably having a *café*.

Patsy shrugged her shoulders, as if to say, "So what's two hours in this wonderful place?" We ambled back through the village. Patsy wanted to buy some postcards; she planned to use them as a visual aid, along with her photographs (in the end, she took probably a dozen rolls), for a lecture she planned to give about her trip. The decision over the best views took up nearly a half hour. I'd always avoided souvenir shops, but found myself suddenly fascinated by all the kitschy stuff. I found myself looking for a key chain with a plastic Black Virgin, and ended up buying a Rocamadour ballpoint pen with pink ink and a cellophane package of glazed walnuts, which were among the usual *produits régionaux*.

I suggested a *citron pressé*. We found a quiet little café. A *citron pressé* is superior to a lemonade. It is civilized and refined, like high tea served in the classic tradition. One is presented with a tall glass on a china saucer, containing the juice of a couple of freshly squeezed lemons. Alongside is a sugar pot, a pitcher of cold water, and a spoon. You add water and sugar to taste, and stir it up. It's fresh and tangy, but it's the ritual that makes it elegant.

As the time neared four o'clock we strolled back to the ramparts. The buses were still empty; only a few early stragglers had made their way back. I approached the group of drivers again. The driver of the bus that had Charleston locked in was on hand. He admonished me for my error, more dutifully than contemptuously. I pleaded with him to move the bus and sensed a weakening in his armor. I pointed to Patsy, who was happily munching the glazed walnuts with one eye on the offerings of the souvenir shop, and explained that she was a visiting friend whom I was attempting to show as much of the country as possible. We had already been delayed several hours as a result of my ignorance of the regulations.

He hailed a fellow driver—the driver of the bus parallel to his. They crossed the road and mounted their buses. As soon as this exercise began I realized the enormity of my request. Villages like Rocamadour were not built to accommodate giant tour buses. It would have been one thing if the drivers were simply departing in single file up the road. But freeing Charleston meant that the first bus had to turn down toward the village at an angle in the tiny street (there were three other buses parked parallel to his), so that the second driver could pull up the road and back down again in the space deserted by the first bus. Charleston, freed, looked the size of a ladybug. Patsy and I hopped in. There were now literally inches of space on either side of the car, between the stone rampart and the wall of the bus. This delicate operation brought forth the entire pack of drivers, who guided me, inch by inch, through the opening. I was sweating, fearful of denting Charleston; Patsy was craning her neck out the window. Finally, we were clear. I got out and thanked all the drivers for this enormous favor. Patsy, no stranger to New York, where a similar situation might have elicited rude behavior, was equally impressed by their helpfulness.

Through Patsy's eyes, sights I'd seen time and again took on their original wonder. The *gouffre de Padirac*, an enormous chasm in the limestone massif of Gramat, seemed even more awesome. The deep caverns are reached by descending in two elevators to passageways with astonishing stalagmites that can be seen both on foot and by boat along the underground river three hundred and thirty-eight feet below the surface. Both Patsy and I, being from Missouri, are stalagmite—and stalactite—buffs: the underground caves of Meramec Caverns and Onondaga Cave in the Ozarks are renowned. Padirac has a powerfully dramatic setting and a legend connected to it, involving a Faustian bargain struck between St. Martin (and his mule) and Satan (with his sack of souls). Patsy, who had read Butler's *Lives of the Saints*, strictly for amusement, relished all such lore.

Though I'd been to Padirac at least three or four times, I'd never seen it under more treacherous conditions. Patsy, to my surprise, proved amazingly intrepid. Because of the severe floods during the spring and summer of

1993, the river was a gushing, roiling torrent. We could hardly hear ourselves speak above its roaring turbulence as we trundled down steep wooden stairs sloshing with water. The water pelted us from overhead. The smooth, timeworn rocks glistened on every side. Passageways underfoot were slippery—a misstep and you could be swept into the surging river. When we boarded the boats *(insubmersibles)*, they rocked nauseatingly. We were both giddy, a nervous giddy. If this had been the States, the caves would have been "closed temporarily due to unsafe conditions." But this was France, the France that loves raw nature.

At the end of the boat excursion, an automatic souvenir photograph is taken of each returning boatload. Patsy and I chose to purchase one, which cost an outrageous eight dollars. When it was mailed to us later, it proved to be worth every penny. Patsy and I are huddled together, frozen and drenched, and—I remembered—fatigued and famished after the ninety-minute excursion. The photograph, however, illuminates the scene like a stage set. The hellish rain and gloomy atmosphere are erased, reducing the crowd in the boat to a cast of comical characters having a seemingly inexplicable reaction to what appears to be a beautiful setting. Patsy and I are smiling cheerily, having survived the reckless adventure together.

A photograph that exists solely in my mind is of Patsy standing on the ramparts of Castelnaud, a castle that bounced back and forth like a tennis ball between French and English hands during the Hundred Years War. It has one of the most spectacular views in all of the region. Patsy felt the ghosts of knights were stalking the land: nothing seemed changed since the Middle Ages. From its dramatic perch high on the hill, you gaze over the Céou valley and the meandering Dordogne River to Beynac Castle in the near distance. Beynac was Castelnaud's formidable rival throughout the Middle Ages. What is astonishing is how *close* the two castles are—how could anybody get a decent night's sleep? In the artillery tower of Castelnaud are displays of armor and weaponry. Those hourglass knights' suits of armor seem so small—size six?—that even I would have a problem with a fit.

Since I'd last been to the castle, they had added a video demonstrating the use of primitive cannons and stone balls. Patsy and I were amazed to learn that a stone ball could be hurled from the contraption built for that purpose—a sort of giant slingshot—the distance of two miles. All the way across Prospect Park, I mentally translated.

As we watched the video a scenario played out in my head. Everyone at Castelnaud is seated around the banquet tables for a feast and evening of merrymaking. *Thonk!* A stone ball lands on the roof! The enemy has attacked and there is general pandemonium. In a movie you would see the tables overturned and a little scrappy dog steal away with a leg of mutton, you would hear the bare-teethed horses whinnying as they're wrenched from the stables and the clatter of their hooves on cobblestones, you would see a bolt of lightning strike from the heavens. The women and children would cluster together and run for shelter, but where? My castle plan doesn't include a broom closet—perhaps they'd flee to the kitchen. The knights and infantry rush to their posts.

How a castle was ever overtaken is beyond me. A common strategic position for a castle is on an outcrop of rock over water, so that it is impenetrable from at least one side. Inland, it would be laid out in defensive rings,

with an outer curtain wall. If, by luck, the enemy penetrated that wall, there would be an inner curtain wall,
which could be two feet thick and thirty-five feet tall.
This design scheme was picked up from Syrian castles by
the Crusaders. In front of this wall would be a draw-
bridge, which could be hoisted to send everybody into the
slimy-green, infested moat. Arrows would be showered
from above through arrow loops, cleverly wedge-shaped
so archers could aim in a range of directions. Troops
storming through the main gate with its great iron port-
cullis would be met with stones hurled from machicola-
tions and boiling water poured from what were called
murder holes cut in the ceiling. I have a problem figuring
out how those huge cauldrons of water could be kept at
a boil. Bottom windows were made small enough so that
the enemy couldn't crawl through. Soldiers manned the
merlons, the intervals between crenellations, topped with
fierce finials. What chance did an intruder have? Better, it
seems to me, to sit it out, starve the bastards.

Castelnaud makes this past a vivid reality.

Patsy and I would spend the end of our days at the
house, with aperitifs before the fire and a candlelit dinner
with wine. It was a time to relax and talk. We know each
other practically as well as we know ourselves, and accept each other for who we are. I am myself—my best
self—with Patsy, a profoundly satisfying feeling.

The Marian Seldes character in Edward Albee's play
Three Tall Women says of middle age: "It's the only time
you get a three-hundred-and-sixty-degree view—see in all
directions. Wow! What a view!" That suggests to me a
woman standing on a mountaintop, at a pinnacle, exhil-

arated. It's not the emotion I would use to describe where I think Patsy and I have arrived. There's more a sense of being grounded, having traversed the proverbial long, bumpy road and arrived at a paved one, which feels easier underfoot. We are realistic, surefooted, grateful for good health and fortune. Friendship—particularly with women friends—is extremely precious to both of us.

Our perennial subjects for conversation are friends, our cats, work, sometimes world and local news, books. Patsy is a voracious reader (on one of our jaunts, she regaled me with the plot of a book by Angela Thirkell, an English writer to whom she had become recently addicted). As a prelude to her France trip, she'd read *The Parkman Reader*, a selection edited by Samuel Eliot Morison of Francis Parkman's 1865 nine-volume *The French and English in North America*. Patsy's enthusiasm for a subject was so contagious that I couldn't wait to get my hands on the tome.

Patsy and I both feel French is in our blood, since our hometown of St. Louis was founded by the French. In 1764, the village was established in honor of Louis IX, who reigned in the thirteenth century. Pierre Laclède, who founded the city, was the scion of a prominent French family—Laclede Station Road, in the suburbs, not far from my old house, is named after him. By late 1764, some fifty families had settled the town that had been studiously laid out by Laclède, with fancy street names like Rue Royale. Patsy said that with her heightened interest in all things French, she had begun to notice the number of French street names—sometimes bastardized, such as Gravois, which in St. Louisese is pronounced Grav-oy, with the accent on the first syllable. Laclède saw the town as a crossroads, and his vision held. It's renowned as the

"Gateway to the West," symbolized in the famous Saarinen arch on the riverfront.

A glass of wine and a fire invited philosophizing. We talked of our lives, of how we felt at this point. Like me, Patsy has never been married. She has a problematic history with men: when they draw closer to commitment, she backs off; when they back off, she grows madly attached. Now, Patsy said, romantic fantasies have receded. She isn't sure if her sexual impulses have faded because of menopause or—she chuckled—simply been replaced by her infatuation with her cat, Ferguson, who is the love of her life.

Being in our fifties, we agreed, is somewhat bewildering. I showed her a poem, titled "The Child," by W. S. Merwin (who lives and works in Southwest France):

> *Sometimes it is inconceivable that I should be the*
> *   age I am*
> *Almost always it is at a dry point in the afternoon*
> *I cannot remember what I am waiting for and in my*
> *   astonishment I*
> *Can hear the blood crawling over the plain*
> *Hurrying on to arrive before dark.*

"It's like having a new suit of clothes that doesn't quite fit, isn't it?" I asked her. People *die* in their fifties. As Merwin says, you feel the blood crawling over the plain: death is conceivable; not frightening, but *possible.*

And will we ever make love again? Patsy shrugged, with a scrunched expression, as if it wasn't beyond the realm of possibility. For myself, I doubt it. You have to seek a passionate relationship, which is not something I do—in fact, I've never felt the sexual drive that a number

of my women friends have—and I don't deceive myself in
thinking that men would find me sexy. If anything, it's not
passion I miss, but being physically touched. I do miss being felt, held, made to feel alive in that way. Patsy understood. The concern is not about making love, but keeping
love going with others.

For the last day of her visit, I asked Patsy if she wanted
to take a day's excursion or just relax at the house. She
preferred the latter. I pulled up the floor heater between
the chairs and we curled up with books for the morning.
Around noon, we drove to Collonges-la-Rouge for lunch.
The small red-sandstone manor houses built by leaders of
the viscountcy of Turenne for their holidays make this
town unique. We walked along the blush-red roads, admiring the blush-red houses. It's as if the town glows
from an inner fire. At a small, rustic restaurant, we shared
a bottle of wine over omelettes and crusty country bread.
It was the end of this journey with Patsy, but the first, I
proposed, as we raised our glasses, of other pilgrimages
together in France.

15

CHIEN MÉCHANT

A daily constitutional is a vital part of my life at the house. I drive to the valley, where the terrain is flat, for a comfortable run. I have mapped out two different routes. One is an eight-kilometer run, flat from start to finish, from the bridge over the Dordogne to the village of Puybrun, where Monsieur Jean Mas, the all-important *notaire*, lives. I walk one way and run back. The road goes past farmhouses and enviable country homes, cornfields, vegetable gardens, cows and goats grazing in meadows. The other, with gentle slopes, follows the Dordogne in the direction of St-Céré. The river is to one side, forest to the other. It's the more solitary route of the two. I can make of it what I will: a 10k, 12k, or whatever.

In the summer of 1986, during a run in Prospect Park one Sunday morning—when the park is closed to traffic—I was struck from behind by a bicyclist zooming along at top speed. I flew into the air and, when I landed, saw that my lower left arm was bent at a very peculiar angle. At the emergency room in a nearby hospital, I found out I'd broken both arms, the left acutely. Even worse, the seriously broken arm was improperly set, so it subsequently had to be rebroken and operated on (for nearly four hours) at the Hospital for Special Surgery in Manhattan. Yes, suffering has its positive side—or so Mother and church had always affirmed. I always got a seat on the subway. I discovered the generosity of friends and grew to accept dependency.

When I started to run in France, however, the following fall, I was in a different frame of mind. What if I was struck by an automobile? What if I was knocked unconscious? Who would know who I was, where I was from? I couldn't shake these troubling thoughts. It occurred to me that it would be wise to carry some sort of identification. Once, during a visit to a monastery in another region, I'd picked up—in an outburst of nostalgia—one of those little Catholic "dog tags," in green felt, which read IN CASE OF EMERGENCY CALL A PRIEST. I rescued it from the back of the drawer of the bureau, where it had lain forgotten. I crossed out the words *a priest* and substituted *Marius Bézamat* and his phone number. I carried it in the pocket of my running pants, and it made all the difference. The vision of myself as a nameless corpse vanished.

When I returned the following spring, Monsieur Bézamat invited me inside the house—he had something to return to me. There on the table was the little dog tag! Evidently, it had fallen out of my pocket on the road. Monsieur Bézamat explained that the people at the Fénelon in Carennac had phoned him, after someone had brought it to them, and he'd stopped by to fetch it. Monsieur Bézamat, my unsuspecting guardian, looked a little sheepish. I pocketed the tag with some embarrassment. The miracle of its return was reassuring, but it also gave me the creeps. It was as if that little tag possessed some Catholic voodoo that still had a hold on me.

Each day on my walk/run I see something different: the particular cast of light or configuration of clouds, the sight of a pheasant in flight, the cycle of crops: tomatoes, squash, pumpkins, corn. On this particular morning—it was a warm October in 1993—I began my walk late in the afternoon, on the day before I was to leave for Paris. At a brisk pace, I passed a country house where an elderly gentleman, a baggy figure in bib overalls, was tending his flower garden. Just past the house I approached a field—"corn as high as an elephant's eye," I sang to myself—when an enormous German shepherd–like dog, with long spindly legs, bounded from the tall stalks—a blur of fur and bared teeth, sailing through the air in a snarling charge. He hurled himself at my feet and sank his teeth into my left calf, as if it were a pork chop. It happened in a flash, but I had the split-second sinking— and surprisingly clearheaded—realization that I'd be out of commission for any walking or running for a while. Then, shock. I screamed crazily over and over—*aieee, aieee, aieee!* The dog slunk back and crouched, eyeing me threateningly. My leg was spurting blood, drenching my sock, flowing into my running shoe. I stood tottering, stunned, and, remembering the gardener, started screaming, "Monsieur! Monsieur!"

Eventually, he heard my shouts. He propped his hoe against a tree and made his way in my direction, with the side-rocking, struggling gait of an elderly, overweight gentleman.

"Le chien, il est à vous?" I bellowed at him. He shook his head—he didn't own the dog—stamping his foot and

waving his arms to shoo the beast away. Then he came to my side.

Robust as he was, he only reached my chin. I flung my arm around his shoulders for support—feeling monstrously tall—and he clasped an arm around my waist. We staggered like two drunks back to his garden, where he deposited me in a tiny wrought-iron chair. My screams had subsided into moans. Visibly shaken, he wrung his hands helplessly. I started wailing again—*"aieee, un médecin!"*—to put fire under him. I felt like a wild raging creature, unable to regain a sense of reason or presence of mind.

He hurried into the house and quickly returned with some gauze, Band-Aids, a strip of cloth. This was futile. I took a sideways glance at my leg and winced at the alarming brilliant-colored flow of blood still pouring from the punctures.

Then, somehow, magically, at this moment when the world seemed to have spun to a halt, a woman appeared. She was small, with coal-black hair and a dark complexion, and she was wearing bedroom slippers. Where had she come from? She was a figure of amazing calm, despite my renewed cries now that I had a second party to whom I could wail.

She and Monsieur had a hurried exchange about what had happened. I detected her French as nonnative. Italian, perhaps, I thought distractedly. Bending down, she told me, in a tone that commanded me to hush, that she would go back for her car and take me to the doctor. She shuffled off, her heelless slippers flapping on the walk. With this, my cries died. I felt drained, oddly bestilled, exhausted. I asked Monsieur—my mind picking at a stray detail—if the woman was Italian.

"Non, Portuguese," he said. *"Mais une bonne voi-*

sine." *But* a good neighbor—there it was again—as if to reassure me that her foreignness did not detract from her reliability.

In a few minutes she was back with a dilapidated small black car. I eased into the front seat, lifting my bad leg with both hands clasped behind the knee. The floor of the car was a clutter of papers, tools, and rags. A thumb-size plastic Virgin was stuck to the dashboard, rosary beads were draped around the rearview mirror, and a pair of broken sunglasses sat in the open ashtray. As we drove off I asked her where she was taking me. To the doctor in Bétaille. Not the emergency room at St-Céré? I pressed her. No, the Bétaille doctor would be best. Was she sure he was there? (This was a Monday.) Yes, he was there. She must have checked. During this limited conversation, I was intrigued by her accent. It suddenly, unaccountably, occurred to me that that's how foreign *I* sounded speaking French, when I couldn't hear the distortion myself.

She drove into the parking lot across from the bakery and stopped the car. I followed her—she made no attempt to assist me—with mincing limps, to an office at the rear of a building, which also housed a butcher and a small grocery. She rang the bell and the door was instantly opened by the young doctor, outfitted in a crisp white coat and with an expectant expression on his face. Once again, this new candidate for my woes set me off: *"un chien méchant,"* I sobbed. He nodded patiently and guided me, with the sort of upright, confidence-building stance typical of doctors, to the examining table. We established that I was American. (The locals can't distinguish, of course, between an American or English accent, and since many British have settled in this area, they are usually surprised at my nationality.) *"Américaine!"* he whispered, as if it were a sacred word. I was probably his first American patient.

"C'est pas très grave," he said reassuringly, and told me to lie back so that he could clean and dress the wound. He asked if I had had a tetanus shot. Yes? Then he would give me a painkiller and an antibiotic, and I should see a doctor as soon as I reached Paris, and then my doctor in New York. The Portuguese woman stood patiently to the side, her crossed arms enclosing her cloth sack purse. *"Regardez, madame,"* the doctor instructed her, as if she were a medical student, pointing out the position of the gashes on either side of my leg made by the eyeteeth and lower teeth, respectively—*"une pîqure classique!"* He beamed at me as if I'd earned a merit badge. When he finished, he patted my leg and I sat up, feeling intact again now that I was bandaged. Since I hadn't brought any money with me, I promised to return and pay him before I left in the morning.

I hobbled stiffly to the car. It was painful to walk, since the dog's eyeteeth had penetrated the muscle. On the drive back to my car, Madame told me in no uncertain terms that I should see the people who owned the dog; they were responsible for the doctor's bill. I dismissed this with a wave of my hand—twenty dollars was the last thing I was concerned about. And anyway, what people? When we reached the car, I thanked her profusely. She had performed the kind service with the unquestioning dutifulness of a soldier. She nodded like a lieutenant dismissing the troops and pulled away.

I drove directly to the Hirondes. I needed to tell them the time of my departure the next morning, but if the truth be told, I was yearning for some sympathy.

Raymond was standing on the porch and looked aghast, just the reaction I wanted, when he saw my bandaged leg and gimpy walk. *"Qu'est-ce qui se passe?"* he wanted to know. When I told him about the dog attack, his lower lip dropped and a blank curtain seemed to fall across his face. For the first time since I'd known him, he was utterly dumbfounded. He waved me inside with an encompassing gesture. *"Simone, Simone,"* he called helplessly.

But you must find the owners, she said instantly, stripping herself of her apron as she came from the kitchen. I smelled and heard the sizzle of roasting potatoes. Raymond wagged his head vigorously in agreement. I said that I wouldn't be able to do that: it was difficult to drive, and where would I begin? Besides, I had to get ready to leave in the morning.

No, Simone insisted. She would go with me, or Raymond, or both of them. The owners must be found, because—the sticking point—they owed me money for the doctor bill! I said that the twenty dollars was not that important to me—I was still looking for a "poor you" and some coddling. But it *was* important, they insisted. Raymond said he would get the car and the two of us would go.

Off we went, to the scene of the crime. The gardener had returned to his pruning. Raymond stopped and got out of the car. The gardener came over and bent down, his ruddy, round face filling the window. I made a little wave—remember me?—and thanked him for all of his help. He tipped his hat and stood back up. Through the open window, I could hear the drift of conversation between the two men.

Hironde: Do you know whose dog this could be?

Gardener: No, never seen the dog. Probably a dog from the hunt.

This was alarming. A hunting dog? I had a horrifying image of diseased fangs, dripping with the blood of wild animals.

Hironde: What would they have been hunting?

Gardener: Rabbits, probably.

Hironde: Not pheasants?

Thus followed a discussion of the hunt, types of guns, vantage points for various game, and so on. The point of our mission seemed to have been lost.

Then Hironde: But would it have been a hunting dog? It's Monday. It's illegal to hunt on Monday.

A shrug from the gardener.

That matter unresolved, they lapsed again into chit-chat: offspring, mutual acquaintances. The light of late afternoon was tinted by the sinking red sun. The valley had a hush about it. I gazed out my window. A few cows, drawn to this bewildering human exchange, meandered to the fence by the car. They stood rooted, as if they would remain there until the end of time. I returned their dull-witted stare. The congregations of insects around their eyes—shouldn't it be madly irritating?—provoked only the merest twitch of an ear or an involuntary ripple of skin. They munched contentedly. The car was warm with the trapped sun. I could hardly keep my eyes open.

Raymond opened the door and slumped into the front seat. He started the motor but made no move to go forward. He announced that he and the gardener had discussed the prospect of going to the magistrates about the dog. He shook his head at the gravity of such an action. If you go to the magistrates, he said, they might simply shoot the dog. (Not a bad idea, I thought wickedly.) That would be too radical, he said, reading my mind. He drummed his hands on the steering wheel, deep in thought. Ah, he finally exclaimed, tapping his forehead with an index finger, we would pay a visit to his friends who lived in the valley and knew all the goings-on. The man was a former policeman.

This aroused a spark of energy in me. Our search was taking on aspects of a detective story. We continued along the same road and then turned off along a backcountry lane, eventually winding around to a farmhouse. Out came a robust woman, approaching the car at a near gallop, arms outstretched in a high-spirited greeting to Raymond. She had a halo of thick curly black hair, penetrating blue eyes that sized me up, and a smooth, milk-white complexion unusual in a farm woman. She was more beautiful for being overweight, wonderfully earthy. I felt diminished by her. She swept us into the house, where we sat at the wooden kitchen table as she poured a rough red wine from a labelless bottle. Immediately, we were joined by her husband, who was as pale and sickly as she was robust and healthy. He was thin to the point of emaciation, his shoulders hunched as if he were in constant pain. His face was craggy and weathered. A wan smile revealed teeth like a decaying picket fence. He sat in a chair near the fireplace, his arms draped languidly over the chair arms with his wrists dangling lifelessly. I wondered if he was seriously ill.

When she heard the story, Madame assured me that country farm dogs were trained to bark and to defend their territory if provoked, but would never attack outright. What did this dog look like? I mentioned its color and size and had hardly gotten the words out when Madame boomed, *"Aha!"* That monster had gone after her on her *vélo*—bike—and she'd barely managed to escape. Then she emitted a bellow of triumph: my brother-in-law's dog! She pounded the table victoriously with a fist.

Madame said that she'd warned her brother-in-law time and again that the dog was a no-good rascal. We must pay him a visit, she insisted, running her hands through her hair as if to tame her exasperation. He owed me the money for the doctor bill!

I must have looked completely startled—she halted in the midst of her outburst when she saw my reaction. I *was* startled—not so much that this was her brother-in-law's dog, but that she'd admitted to it. Apparently, the dog's attack would be more fuel for the fire of a long-standing feud with her brother-in-law. I glanced at her husband, who had lit a cigarette and was dragging on it despondently. For a policeman, he had a curious lack of interest in the case. The energy for any fight seemed to have been sapped from him.

Raymond and I walked back to the car. Dusk was setting in and I was beginning to feel the pangs of hunger. Yet events were moving along inexorably. Though we didn't speak of it, Raymond and I were now in collusion, bound to see this through. We drove a short distance to the farmhouse of the brother-in-law.

Raymond suggested I wait in the car. Presumably, he felt it best for him to approach the people with what had to be a rather delicate matter. To relieve my anxiety, I perused a scruffy paperback guide to mushrooms I discovered in the glove compartment. A good twenty minutes passed. Then Raymond rapped on the window and gestured for me to follow him. I was extremely nervous, not only in the role of accuser, but in having to confront the vicious dog. We passed through the barnyard to a shed, where a portly gentleman with a rubbery red face and scrambled bristly hair stood with a bird-boned woman half his size, whom I took to be his wife. She was that lusty woman's sister? Raymond gestured to me with upturned palm—my American neighbor—as if serving me up. They seemed congenial enough, but something—their nonchalance and placidity—made me vaguely distrustful. We walked to the shed and there, secured with a heavy chain to a post and lying with his giant head resting on his great outstretched paws—looking for all the world like a repentant criminal—was the dog. I nodded and said, chalkily, to Raymond, *"C'est le chien."*

The man asked what the doctor's fee was, without a word of apology for their dog's behavior or inquiry as to my well-being. He withdrew a hundred-franc bill from the wallet in his pants pocket and, folding it twice over as if to make it vanish, slipped it to me, as if we were in some sort of conspiracy. He said—as if to assuage some guilt I might feel—that they would be reimbursed by their insurance company. The whole discussion left me feeling off-kilter; I had the unreasonable sensation that perhaps *I* was culpable.

Suddenly, unbidden, the woman announced that she had driven up to my house with the Portuguese woman. They'd not found me at home, she said tartly. Perversely, I suspected that it was more the tenacity of the Portuguese woman to see that I was repaid than an act of kindness on this woman's part. But I was mystified nonetheless.

How did they know where I lived? I asked her.

She drew her shoulders up to her ears and pouted, with an expression that said I was asking the obvious. Well, the American with the house on the hill . . . It was not the first time I'd discovered myself to be a well-known figure, when I assumed I was anonymous.

As we climbed back into the car Raymond turned to

me and shuddered. *"Il est vraiment un grand chien!"* he said. I swelled, the heroine (as if *I'd* overcome the beast). *"Oui,"* I said boastfully. I commented that the couple had seemed cooperative enough. He confided that they were in some debt to him (how I relished this intrigue). When they'd had some money problems he'd bailed them out. In fact, their farm was now for sale. Did I have any American friends who would be interested?

"Monsieur a trouvé le chien!" I exclaimed to Simone when we reached the house. *"Oui, Simone!"* he said solemnly. Then he launched into an account of his detective work, circling the table in increasing excitement. She brought coffee and motioned to him with a sit-yourself gesture—as if he were an overwrought puppy. As she sipped her coffee her lips were pursed with a tight little expression of satisfaction at the triumph of justice. Monsieur Hironde went to the telephone book and jotted down the name and address of the owners of the dog. I glanced at the florid script: *M. et Me. Maury.* If I should experience any further difficulties, he said, I should contact them.

Later I realized that while I hadn't exactly received the sympathy I'd wanted, I'd certainly gotten consideration all around. Someone could have said that I was foolish—the foolish American—to be walking on a country road defenseless, so what should I expect?

They could have defended their own, against the foreigner, and let it go at that. In the end, however, their reactions seemed instinctive. The matter was simple: I was owed money. And owing money was no small matter, according to simple country justice. It was recompense, not sympathy, that the victim was due.

The next morning I packed up and closed the house. In

Bétaille, I stopped at the doctor's office to pay the bill and ask for a change of dressing. He commented that it was a good thing we'd located the owners of the dog—word travels faster than the post here. He wished me well and gave me his card.

On my next trip, I met an engaging young South African couple, Gavin and Lillian Bell, acquaintances of the Servais, who compounded my distrust of country dogs. They were managing a small *auberge* near Salvignac for a friend who had gone back to South Africa to invest in a trout farm. When I visited them on a Saturday afternoon, Gavin had a dog story that topped mine. He was cycling along a nearby country road and came upon a freshly killed sheep, its throat savagely ripped open. Then another. And another. Finally, after passing nine dead sheep, all killed in the same manner, he came upon an Alsatian—"something like your German shepherd," he said—in the throes of its tenth kill. The dog was drenched with blood. At Gavin's approach, it ran off. Gavin found the owner of the sheep, who instantly guessed the owner of the dog. The owner of the sheep dumped his murdered flock on the doorstep of his neighbor and demanded payment for the lot—a tidy sum. The dog owner paid up. Then the sheep owner followed up with a further ultimatum: he would gladly shoot the dog or the owner could send him away. The dog presently resides in Paris.

At this point, I was counting myself lucky—I could have been taken for a sheep—and resolved to meet the problem head-on. I consulted with Simone and Raymond about taking a different route—Bétaille *aller et retour*. Simone knew of no *chien méchant* in this vicinity. But Raymond winced and whispered to her under his

breath, *"Mais on ne sais jamais, Simone."* I asked
Raymond if one could find a *"gaz qui font les larmes,"*
my bumbling attempt at a term for a teargas gun. The
light dawned and he exclaimed at the cleverness of this
idea. *Gaz lacrymogène.* He found a scrap of paper—
the flap of an envelope (all envelopes are saved for just
such purposes)—and wrote down the words to present
at the shop for *la chasse* in Bretenoux. *Une bombe
de défense!* He snorted gleefully. Simone looked less
enthusiastic.

I practiced the word, *lacrymogène*, and entered the
shop. The owner was discussing fishing gear with two
gentlemen and paused for my request. I hoped this would
not appear untoward; I suddenly felt burdened with my
identity as the American woman with the house on the
hill. *"Gaz lacrymogène? Bombe de défense?"* I said in
low tones. Question mark, question mark—trying out the
untested, I'm always afraid I won't be understood. But
this was taken, surprisingly, as a matter of course. The
man produced a little capsule, just the right size to grip in
a hand. Armed with my *bombe*, I headed home.

On the patio, I gingerly removed the little red plastic
lever, per instructions, and pushed the indented button
with my index finger. *Pffft*, it worked perfectly. I read the
fine print on the capsule, which contained a rather
strange bit of information: *Sa formule est spécifique pour
une utilisation en lieu clos (clubs, discothèques, etc.).*
(This formula is designed for indoor use.) Nothing about
dogs. The next time I saw Raymond, I showed him my
bombe de défense and pointed out the baffling note. He
looked perplexed, then perturbed. He took a moment before saying lamely, *"Mais il y a des chiens dans les dis-
cos."* And he wasn't joking—dogs go everywhere with

their owners in France. Poor man. I suspect he'd rather me think there were vicious dogs than mad Frenchmen in the country's nightclubs.

So I take the Bétaille route, my handy *bombe* at the ready. *Je suis prête pour la bête*—ready for the beast.

16

NOT A
DROP TO DRINK

My concern about weather generally amounts to no
more than wondering if I should carry an umbrella to
work. For my neighbors, however, such matters have a
greater import. More of their lives are spent outdoors:
gardening, drying laundry, marketing. When I depart in
the fall, I sense their despondency at the onset of winter,
which will keep them housebound. In the spring they turn
their faces unconsciously and gratefully to the sun. On
each return visit I receive an update on the previous winter or summer. The October 1991 report: a summer of
drought.

It was a Sunday morning. I had had a long run along
the river road and had just finished up a rich brunch of
large slabs of golden Armagnac-scented French toast,
country bacon, steaming black coffee. I had planned to
take a little afternoon excursion and hurried to wash up
the dishes.

When I turned on the faucet, it coughed, gurgled, and sputtered. I turned it off—a little air pocket, a glitch, whatever, I thought—and tried again. This time there was no cough, but a gasping and hissing, as if it was drawing a last breath. And so it was. There was no water. The cistern, I realized, had run dry. And, of course—the bitter little pill—it *would* be a Sunday.

I resurrected "Points on the Obvious and Obscure." I quickly scanned passages under the heading of WATER:

> The cistern in the Cave holds about 1,200 gallons of rainwater, and is entirely supplied by water from the roof. Therefore, care must be taken not to use more than is really necessary. Unrestricted flushing is discouraged.
>
> The basin, shower, and WC discharge into a septic tank in the Cave which seems to work well as not much washing water goes down. It discharges through a long drain over the edge of the ravine at foot of garden.

Not a word on droughts.

I rooted around for the Pinckney letter, which I hadn't reread for years, hoping to glean something there. What I found only unnerved me:

> I feel I ought to give you some information about the drains, dull though it may be. The sink discharges over a gully which is connected to a three-inch plastic pipe discharging well down the slope, so should never give any trouble. There is a four-inch drain connecting the WC to the fosse septic; the overflow from this goes into a four-inch pitch fibre socketed drain discharging at the far end of the garden. This drain we relaid our-

selves, as it was done so badly by the French. The shower and basin connect direct to the four-inch drain, thus bypassing the fosse septic. Under a flat stone outside, the cave door covers a small rodding eye (a device unknown to the French). Be careful when you leave the house for the winter to draw off the water in the pan; we failed to do this once, with the result that the water froze and burst the side of the pan. There is a filter over the cistern in the cave which ought to be cleaned out every now and then, as it gets filled up with leaves; anyway it prevents them getting into the tank.

What was a "fosse septic"? What was a "pitch fibre socketed drain"? "Rodding eye"? It left me shaken.

What to do? Who to call? I decided to award this problem to the Hironde Rescue Squad. I stifled my reluctance to call on them on a Sunday—the day of the big midday meal with friends or relatives—and walked to their house. Luckily, they had no company and had just finished their lunch.

Raymond took it all in stride. In fact, he seemed energized, after his nap-inducing meal. Immediately he was on the phone to the fire department, *les pompiers*. This seemed a dramatic solution, to my mind. Fire engines in Manhattan are a constant and terrifying presence. I'm accustomed to their wailing part in the general cacophonic backdrop, but when one carooms right past, blaring its dizzying alarm, I quake. I picture flames licking at windows, mothers clutching babies and leaping to their deaths. A fire is one of my worst fears. There is a frequently mentioned figure in our family, a Great-Aunt Mary, who was said to have saved every one of her dozen children from their burning house. The story, and Mary herself, had taken on the dimensions of legend. In the family album that I inherited after my mother died, there is a photogravure of an unidentified, staunch-looking woman surrounded by her brood, to whom I've attached this tale of heroism.

Wasn't a dried-up cistern a rather mundane matter for the fire department? Raymond's decision seemed an over-reaction—but mine was not to question why.

While Simone and I carried on a distracted conversation—the trials of the summer's drought—I overheard his account to the man at the other end of the phone: his neighbor, an American woman, had a *maison secondaire;* the cistern had run dry. Pause. No, the house was not attached to the town's water system. Pause. *"Une heure et demi? D'accord."*

A great wave of relief swept over me. Help was on the way within an hour and a half! I applauded. Raymond proceeded to give the firemen directions to both his house and mine, concluding with his phone number. He hung up. The firemen were in Cahors, he explained. Cahors, an hour's drive away! What if my house *had* been on fire?

Then he sat down, with a self-important lift of his shoulders. Assuming the grave avuncular look my problems sometimes elicited, he said that perhaps I should consider hooking up to the local system. Then I would avoid this problem, and my tap water would be drinkable. The initial investment was high, he said, but the yearly fee negligible.

"Oui, ce n'est pas le Moyen Âge," I said jocularly. It did seem smarter than relying on this antiquated system based on iffy rainwater.

So—he slapped the table—I was to return home to await the firemen. He wasn't sure if they would arrive at my house or theirs.

I diddled about the house for well over an hour and a half. Then doubts began to needle my mind. Where were they? Why not run, really *run*, over to the Hirondes; I would meet the firemen head-on if they were close, and could maybe put through another call if they were not. Just to see if they were on the way. Just to see that they weren't lost, or had the wrong phone number.

About halfway down the road to the Hirondes, moving at a steady clip, I heard the roar of a car behind me and a repeated honking. It was the Servais. Madame rolled down the window and shouted excitedly that the firemen had arrived at my house and, finding no one home, had come to their house! She'd called Hironde, who was on his way! *"Allez! Vite! Vite!"* She rolled up the window, and they sped off in a cloud of dust.

Damnation. The afternoon had turned into a sort of Toad motorcar chase out of *The Wind in the Willows*, everyone tearing up the roadways in mad circles. I ran for home.

A sparkling, cherry-red fire truck—looking like a very large toy you'd find under the Christmas tree—was parked in the drive. Several firemen were unraveling the fire hose, with Raymond in the lead. When he saw me, he raised his arms in grateful salutation.

"La cave," I shouted. *"C'est ouvert!"*

The firemen trundled into the *cave*. I drew Raymond aside. The flurry of officious activity made me wonder about the cost. *"Vraiment rien,"* he said—nothing really—but, with a shuffling of the fingers, indicated that a tip for the men would be in order.

He bowed and said he would be off, with a slight mock mopping of the brow suggesting the strenuous activity he'd been through. I waited on the patio while the firemen filled the cistern in the *cave*, pondering the delicate matter of the tip. Having never called on firemen to refill a cistern, I couldn't imagine what amount to offer. There were three of them, one who was apparently the supervisor and two younger men. Too little (ten dollars?) would be resented. Too much (forty dollars? fifty dollars?) might appear ugly-Americanish. I eventually settled on five dollars apiece—fifteen dollars.

The men tramped out of the cave, looking oversized in their great slickers, hats, and boots—especially for this rather minor task. They wound the hose back on the truck; the whole thing had taken no more than a half hour. The supervisor advised me not to turn on the taps for several hours, in order to let the water settle in the cistern.

I asked him, feigning ignorance, what I owed them for the service.

"*Gratuit,*" he said graciously.

Now was the time to offer compensation. I smiled faintly, feeling embarrassed and awkward—especially being a woman making this somewhat crude gesture. There are some things better left to men. "*Pour votre ennui,*" I said, slipping him the money.

The lagniappe seemed to have struck the right note.

Thus began a seemingly never-ending effort to connect the house to the local water system. I started at the *mairie* in Carennac, which, I discovered, is open on a limited basis. It is a rather stately but plain little building, set off from the main road next to the elementary school. Class was in session and I took the occasion to peek in the window. Some two dozen children were seated at their desks, reciting grammar drills. Their voices drifted like a muffled hymn through the windows. Their number surprised me. I'd never seen children on the streets in Carennac, a fact that contributed to the village's placid atmosphere. I had seen kids on surrounding country roads, walking along with their *copains*—their buddies—or standing alone outside a house, waiting for transport. Where did they come from? How did they get here? I had no idea how the elementary-school system worked in the country.

A stout, pretty woman, with a budlike mouth and the merest hyphens of eyebrows, rose from her desk when I entered the *mairie*. Her name was Madame Claudine Sanchez; her husband was Spanish. I explained that I was the owner of Pech Farguet, to which she nodded knowingly. The water system established by the former owners, I said, was inadequate. The Pinckneys, she assented in recognition. (Once again I was struck by the villagers' knowledge about the particulars of Pech Farguet.) Not only was I unable to drink or cook with tap water, but the drought had been *une catastrophe*. The solution was to connect my house to the municipal water system. How was I to proceed?

She came around the counter and led me to a table where enormous maps were mounted in metal racks and covered in plastic. With some difficulty, she eventually found the proper map. It was on a minute scale, such as the incredible *série orange* maps done by the Institut Géographique National that I keep at the house. Each and every domicile is recorded with an infinitesimal square smaller than the head of a pin. We hovered over the map. She pointed a bright red fingernail to Magnagues. My eyes traveled down the spiderweb line representing the road to the Hirondes' house, then back up the road to the fork: to the left the Bézamats, to the right

Pech Farguet. A little ant on the map, but there it was, my house. It was *on record*, verifiable, official, on the town-hall map!

She circled back to the counter. Surveyors would have to investigate the property and determine the location of the pipelines—she believed they weren't far—to which my house could be hooked up. The next step was to write a letter to Saur, the company in Figeac, who would do the job. They would then be able to give me an estimate of the cost. Here we go, I thought. I coughed apologetically. I was not too adept at writing letters in French, I said, especially one that required technical explanations. Could she possibly compose the letter for me?

She glanced at her watch. It was almost noon. Lunch was beckoning. This presented a real conflict. *"Alors"*— she sighed—and drew out a piece of blank paper. Her letter was brief and straightforward, with just a brushstroke of formal French circumlocution. *"J'ai l'honneur de vous demandez le rattachement à ce réseau."* (It is an honor for me to ask you for the connection of this network.) *Voilà!* Letter in hand, I went home for lunch and that afternoon sent off my copy.

After a trip in the early spring of 1992—when I put through a call to inquire if my correspondence had come to anyone's attention—I received a letter from Saur in New York, with a detailed two-page document setting forth the procedures that would be necessary for the *branchement*—the connection—as well as a printed folder with thirty articles devoted to the *Service des eaux* in the *département du Lot*. The estimate for the job was more than I'd anticipated. Yet, on the other hand, it didn't seem an outrageous amount for such a major undertaking.

Expenses for the house are minimal. I pay two taxes each year: *taxes foncières* and a *taxe d'habitation*. I have a basic Assurances Mutuelles de France with Groupe Azur, in Bretenoux, which covers fire and theft. The gas-and-electricity bill is automatically deducted from my BNP account twice a year. I try to keep some reserve funds in my bank account for the unexpected (one year a section of the roof needed repair). There is no phone bill to pay; it seems simpler to stop at the Carennac post office to make a call than having the expense and going through the rigmarole of paying bills. And, in truth, I prefer being phoneless, televisionless, radioless—out of touch, living a step back in time. Generally, Pech Farguet is like a little fort and percolates along at its own pace.

After the initial expenditure for the installation, the bill for water would be quite reasonable, according to the Hirondes. A drop in the bucket, so to speak, and well worth it. For that I would save buying bottled water and trips to the Salges' well. Friends had also pointed out that if and when I decided to sell the house—fat chance—this would be an important factor in its favor.

The contract was terribly complicated; in fact, impenetrable. *"Je préfère qu'on parle en personne,"* I wrote back. I explained that I would be coming to France in the fall, when I would come to the Gramat office to discuss the particulars.

In October, I went to Gramat. After many inquiries I eventually found the tiny office of Saur on a little back street behind the cathedral. I tapped on the door.

"Entrez!"

Seated at the only desk was a strikingly handsome man in his thirties.

"Monsieur Carsac?" I ventured, hardly expecting this to be the man attached to the letter.

"Oui, je vous attend," he said, as if we'd had an appointment that very minute. There was a deadly professionalism about him—not a crack in his demeanor.

He began riffling through papers on his desk. He'd not been able to find the right map for my house, he mumbled, and then threw up his hands, as if he was always ambushed by this sort of problem. Well, we could proceed anyway. He wasn't sure when the work could be done—maybe July, maybe August. He raised his hand to chin level, indicating an invisible stack of papers on his desk.

I informed him that I would sign the contract and wanted to go ahead and pay for the work. This would surely set things in motion (such expeditiousness would be my inclination, not that of the French, I should have realized). Would Monsieur accept my French-franc traveler's checks (I'd come prepared with extra money to pay for the work on this trip)? Not possible, he said sternly. But, I explained, since the checks were in French francs, it was exactly like cash. His nose twitched, as if this was a further irritation. The bank was just a few blocks away, he said.

I ran to the bank. Why am I forever trying to beat the noon closing of everything in France? I cashed the wad of traveler's checks, studying the young woman's face to see if she registered surprise. I hoped no other customer was observing the mound of bills being counted—I fantasized a gun at my back as soon as I walked out the door. The idea of carrying so much cash, even for a few blocks, made me extremely nervous. I sped back to the Saur office.

I signed the two copies of the contract. I counted

out and recounted the precise amount of francs. Monsieur Carsac counted and recounted them. Eventually—Monsieur waiting it out—I dug out the last centime. *Fini.*

In June of 1993, I called Monsieur Carsac from the booth at the Carennac post office and was told that work on my house had been postponed. In short, my house was creeping up on their to-do list. A month after I got back to New York, I received an amended *facture* or bill from Saur. The cost had risen slightly, based on a more recent estimate. I paid the difference.

N₀, Monsieur Bézamat told me in October 1993, the work had not been started. His expression was pained, as if he shared some responsibility for the delay. I should call the Saur office. Before I made my shopping rounds in St-Céré, I stopped at the post office to put through a call to Gramat. No answer. And of course the office would be closed the next day, as well as Monday, France's usual day off. I hung up in a fury. I would be spending the following week in the Auvergne. A delay here for me wasn't a matter of days, but months and months, until my next visit. "*Merde,*" I muttered.

When I received a *facture* from Saur at the end of January in New York, I took it as a positive sign. The bill was for the "*1er semestre*" of service. Then, at the end of May, just before I planned to return, there was a second bill for the same amount. (The Hirondes had underestimated slightly.) We were in business at last!

And so, when Monsieur Bézamat greeted me upon my arrival with a "*problème,*" I was incredulous. He offered to follow me directly to the house. He parked the car, slammed the door, and stood poised for a moment, hands on hips—a momentary reluctance to deliver bad news. Then he advanced and pointed out to me the placement of the *compteur*, the underground meter. It was entrenched on the far side of the incline leading up to the garage, in the shadow of my rosemary bush at the edge of the woods. Which is to say, it was a far stretch from the *cave*. In short, Monsieur Bézamat informed me, it was an impossible task for Monsieur Bru—who had moved into the post of plumber after Monsieur Prysbil was taken to a sanatorium—to make a connection from the *compteur* to the cistern. He would not only have to dig a tunnel for a considerable distance but burrow under the stone wall surrounding the house. In other words—the light was dawning—I had the *compteur*, and in Saur's view, the job was done. The bills, of course, would keep coming—the meter, true enough, was installed. Yet it was inoperable: there was no umbilical cord from meter to house.

The *compteur*, Monsieur Bézamat stated, would have to be moved, preferably inside the stone wall opposite the *cave*. Why hadn't Saur consulted with him? he muttered. (I had given the Saur office his name in my absence.) If he'd been informed, he would have advised them. He whistled in disgust.

I was too weary. This being early Friday evening, there would be no recourse until the Saur offices opened on Tuesday. I told Monsieur Bézamat that I would drive to the headquarters in Figeac then and present the problem. After opening the house, I drove down to the well—the old routine—for water.

On Monday evening, when I came home, there was a note on the back of an envelope in Monsieur Bézamat's elegant script under the door. *"Demain matin, avant*

d'aller à Figeac, passez me voir, au sujet du compteur."
(Come see me about the meter.) I noted, slightly shocked,
that it was addressed familiarly: to Ann and signed
Charles.

When I stopped at the house in the morning, he said
that he'd had a sudden brainstorm: the *compteur* was on
public property, not *chez moi*! True or not—I had a mud-
dled notion that perhaps it was indeed on my land, but
was not about to dig up the deeds. This was a stroke of
genius on his part; it would make for an unassailable
argument in my favor! Saur would *have* to move the
compteur. I complimented him on his clever thinking.
Did he truly believe this, or was he just being wily? I
didn't care.

The woman behind the desk in the Saur office, harried
though she was, was persuaded by my argument and
sympathetic with my plight. After a series of phone calls,
she said that they would send a man to the house that
evening, a Monsieur Singe from Puybrun, who had done
the installation. Would six o'clock be agreeable?

On the way home, I stopped at the *alimentation*—the
grocery store—in Carennac on another bit of business.
Monsieur Bézamat had advised mounting a screen around
the chimney to prevent further invasions of *hiboux,
martres*, and company. Monsieur Coussil, whose shop I
lean on at times like the Yellow Pages, was likely to know
the whereabouts of the roofer (Jean Prunet, who had repaired my roof, had passed away). With his customary
passivity, he recommended Monsieur Massalve, who lived
up the road at the end of the village.

My rap on the door set off a feisty yipping and angry
clawing. A young girl with pale white skin and curly
black hair looked at me with painful shyness. I identified

myself and explained the problem. She hushed the dog, who trotted away, mission accomplished, and ushered me into the hall. Could her father stop by the house? I asked.

"*Il est mon mari*," she corrected me softly. I could barely squelch my astonishment—she looked all of twelve years old! Yes, she said, her husband could come by on Friday evening. Indicative of her reclusiveness, she seemed ignorant of the location of my house. She pulled out a map from the chest in the hall so I could point it out.

From there, I swung by the Bézamats. Without hesitation, Monsieur said he would come to the house at six to meet the Saur man.

Monsieur Singe was a ruggedly handsome man with a football-tackle physique, perhaps in his forties. Introductions were made all round.

"*Vous expliquez*," I said, turning the podium over to Monsieur Bézamat immediately. When the incontrovertible fact was presented—that the *compteur* was on public property and would have to be moved—Monsieur Singe became livid. He smacked his forehead, he paced steamily in circles, he pounded a fist on the trunk of his car. Two *days*, two *days*, he'd spent on this job, and now it had to be undone! More storming about. I hovered by the picnic table. Say nothing, an inner voice advised. Look innocent, but look resolute. When Monsieur Singe wound down enough to carry on with the discussion, Monsieur Bézamat steered him to the spot inside the stone wall where the *compteur* should logically have been placed to begin with.

Monsieur Singe rebelled. That would be impossible, he exclaimed, with much gesticulation. That would mean going under the stone wall! He turned on me. The stone wall was ancient, unstable. It would collapse, and then what? I pretended not to speak the language. (He had a point, I feared.) The stone wall, which was approximately six feet high, was constructed of slabs of stone, layered horizontally and highly irregularly, knitted together somewhat magically without the benefit of stabilizing mortar. Monsieur Bézamat, meanwhile, strode to the *cave* and emerged with a metal rod. He plunged it into the ground by the wall, testing the depth of the stones beneath the surface. He proposed that if Monsieur Singe saw fit to reposition the *compteur* outside the wall, he would dig the trench beneath it. This mollified Monsieur Singe not the least. He marched up to the garage and pounded on the stone wall. Why not drill a hole here, through the wall, leading into the *cave*? he shouted insanely. Then the *compteur* could simply be moved to the other side of the rosemary bush, *chez moi*. He bounded down to the *cave*, trailed by Monsieur Bézamat. This seemed a sickening alternative, violating the house, the ancient walls. Better, I said when they returned, that the stone wall crumble than the house fall down. I could have wept.

The detestable Monsieur Singe, with his bullying, hot-tempered manner, stood rooted in front of me and planted his fists on his hips. Intuitively, I knew that he was the type of man who would respond to cajoling and flattery, especially from a woman, but I couldn't bring myself to do it. I explained that I was leaving on a two-day excursion. I needed to think it over. Could he return on Friday, when we could make a final decision? He shrugged and snickered, as if he didn't care if we made an appointment a year from now. Five-thirty? I proposed. Five-thirty, he mimicked. (An inner voice said, he'll keep you waiting, he may not even show up, he's going to make you pay.)

Monsieur Bézamat and Monsieur Bru subsequently

agreed to come by the following Friday. Monsieur Bézamat arrived at the stroke of five-thirty. We sat on the
patio. He seemed pensive.

What is it? I asked.

He swept off his cap, freeing up a thought that had obviously been weighing on his mind.

Aren't you afraid doing what you're doing alone, a single woman? he asked, with the look of fatherly concern
he sometimes gave me.

I couldn't imagine what had provoked this. (Unless he
thought Monsieur Singe was going to steal up in the night
and do me in.) After all these years of *n'ayez pas peur*s,
perhaps it had taken all this time for him to dare to ask.

No, I said, I'm not afraid. It seems very safe here.

But there are not very many women who would do
this, he said.

"*Oui,*" I said. "*Mais être seule—c'est mon tempéra-
ment.*" That seemed to satisfy him.

Monsieur Bru arrived. He is an athletic man in his
forties, prematurely bald, with deep-set eyes and a year-
round nut-brown complexion that gives him a rather feral
appearance. He reviewed the options with Monsieur
Bézamat: the repositioning of the *compteur*, either inside
or outside the wall, versus drilling through the house. After prolonged discussion, measuring, and examination of
the wall, they agreed that drilling through the house was
senseless. And, if Monsieur Singe refused to place the
compteur within the stone wall, they would be able to
deal with it. Monsieur Bru stated that I should not pay
Saur any *supplément* for the extra work.

It was past six o'clock. They left. Here we go again, I
thought miserably: the Saur office would be closed the
next day and Monday, and I was taking the early-
morning train for Paris on Tuesday. It was going to be an-

other aggravating delay. I went in to shower and start dinner.

At seven, Monsieur Singe showed up. I reminded him that we had agreed on five-thirty and that Monsieur Bézamat and Bru had come and gone. No apologies, no explanation. We stood on the patio like two boxers facing off in the ring. I explained that Monsieur Bru found it impracticable to drill through the house. Perhaps Monsieur Singe would consider dropping by his house; the two of them could resolve the question of the placement of the *compteur*. Monsieur Bru, I added lightly, lived nearby.

"Je sais où il est," he said contemptuously. *"Il est un copain."* They'd gone to school together. The two of them pals? I found this hard to believe.

As for the payment for the additional work, how was I going to take care of that? he wanted to know. There was going to be an additional charge of a hundred and sixty dollars.

I stammered. If I refused to pay, the whole business might be stalled again. Yet it seemed unjust, another bundle of money for something that was the company's error. This was unfair, I said, testing the waters. He jerked backward, as if I'd punched him in the stomach. Monsieur Singe was like a tricky fish on a line; he could be reeled in temptingly close to a landing, but then would spin out into the depths. Should I mention Monsieur Bru's counsel that I shouldn't pay more, or would that be a betrayal? When I did, he shouted that Bru had no right to interfere in his business arrangements! So much for his *copain*. He spun on his heels, as if the discussion, such as it was, was closed.

"Alors, je vous payerai!" I shouted in desperation to his retreating back, my fist in the air.

At which point a young man, seemingly from out of

nowhere, approached the patio. In the heat of the moment I hadn't even noticed his car pull in. He looked aghast at having stumbled into this unpleasantness. Monsieur Singe stopped in his tracks. I lowered my clenched fist and swallowed my exclamation.

"Massalve," he announced shyly. The roofer. Instantly, I saw that he was the perfect match for his young wife. He looked the quintessential angelic flower child, tall and lean, with a halo of black curls, the poetic mustache and beard of an aesthete, and deep blue eyes. From my peripheral vision, I saw that his car was painted a bright purple, like a heavenly chariot. He extended his slender hand to Monsieur Singe, who responded with a quick, wrenching handshake. Monsieur Singe then seized the moment to beat a retreat.

Massalve. His very name was a balm. My emotions turned on a dime: from heated anger and frustration to sweet delight. The tension oozed out of my body into a pool on the patio. Monsieur Massalve gazed at the roof. I invited him into the house in order to show him the violation: *caca* that had accumulated just in the past day or so on the newspaper I'd spread in the fireplace. (Monsieur Bézamat's sleuthlike ways are contagious.) Monsieur Massalve bent over and craned his head under the chimney. He righted himself and nodded sympathetically. It was an easy solution, he said. He would mount a *grille* around the chimney and that should solve the problem.

Off he went. I was becalmed. I refused to think any more about Singe and the *problème*. I got out my binoculars and stood on the patio, training them on the cows feeding in the Salgues' barn in the valley, an idyllic sight. The faint clanging of their bells against the troughs carried up the hill. Evening was closing in.

* * *

No one was at home at the Bézamats' when I arrived to pick up the keys in October. By prior agreement in such an event, I found them secreted under the metal milk container on the stone ledge by the front door. Bobbie was beside himself, confounded as to how he ought to behave. He recognized me, yet he was duty bound to defend the property in his family's absence. As I mounted the stairs he rolled on his back on the grass, his tail wagging, all the while growling ferociously.

When I pulled into the house, I noticed that the grassy area in front was churned up, as if it had been plowed. The *compteur* was not by the road. I walked up the hill and stood on the patio. The *compteur*, miracle of miracles, had been relocated to the most desirable position, within the stone wall and within reach of the *cave*. This was beyond belief. I'd come steeled for the next round with Saur and here it was, a *fait accompli*.

This had to be Monsieur Bézamat's doing. But how had he accomplished such a feat? The next morning I stopped at his house, a bottle of wine in hand. He was tinkering in the garage. I saluted him, with the wine bottle raised on high in victory. He came forward, with a shy smile of satisfaction, the cat who'd swallowed the canary.

I grasped his hand and shook it vigorously. And how had he done it?

He placed his bottle of wine on the hood of the car and nonchalantly tucked his hands in his back pockets. He'd driven to Figeac, he explained offhandedly, and stopped at the main bureau of Saur.

You drove to *Figeac*! I exclaimed. It was nearly an hour's drive.

Well, he had had a little business of his own there, he said dismissively.

You spoke to the *chef du centre*! I went on, incredulous.

He nodded sagely. *"Eh, voilà."* The bureau chief had had to face the fact that the *compteur* wasn't on my property. There was no choice but to rectify the situation. He shrugged at the overriding and obvious logic of this position.

I was dumbstruck that he would have put himself out to such a degree. I had underestimated his fidelity.

He ignored my astonishment and urged me to arrange with Bru to proceed with the *branchement*. He tipped his hat and took a half step back, reminding me, as I slid into the car, not to press on the gas pedal when I started the car. (He had witnessed me do this on occasion, resulting in the engine being flooded.)

Monsieur Bru stopped by that evening. Between him and Bézamat, he said, the job would be finished in the spring, without fail. Bézamat would dig the trench and he would follow up with the connection to the cistern. He smiled broadly and gave me a reassuring clap on my shoulder, the first intimate gesture he'd ever made. Now that the job was in familiar hands, my doubts dissolved. Water, water, everywhere—come spring.

17

HOUSE RESEARCH

The dictionary's definition of identity is the "sameness of essential or generic character in different instances." Yet geographical identity can be an elusive thing. If I were asked in New York where I was from, I would reply, "St. Louis." If I were somewhere else in the United States and was asked where I was from, I would say New York. But if I were on Mars, it wouldn't dawn on me to say I was from Carennac, France. For though I now feel at home, I will never feel indigenous. Nor would I ever contemplate moving to France permanently, as people suspect when they discover I have a house there. Eventually I hope to spend more time at Pech Farguet, however. It's constantly beckoning. As soon as I get back to New York from a trip to France, I'm dreaming and planning of when I can go back.

At some point my two worlds took on a seamlessness. Buying the car contributed to a sense of belonging. I no longer felt like a visitor. Charleston gave me permanence.

Life in New York now flows easily into life in France. I don't have to make a pack list anymore. It has become routine. About a month or so in advance of a trip, I book the usual Air France flight, leaving Newark on Thursday evening at six-thirty P.M. and returning two weeks later from Orly at ten-thirty A.M. I have figured out how to get to and from the Paris airport for the price of the *métro*, and know by heart the usual hours for the departures of the train leaving Paris from Austerlitz and returning from St-Denis. The arrangement with Raymond goes like clockwork. My initial feeling of awkwardness and indebtedness to my neighbors has long vanished. We are friends.

And, after twelve years, the house has become like a pair of well-worn shoes that now comfortably fit the contours of my feet. But, unlike a pair of old shoes, Pech Farguet has its own presence and soul. When I close up the house after a visit, I take one last look around and bid a silent *good-bye, house*. It is a living, breathing sentinel that awaits my return. It saddens me to leave it alone and I fear something will befall it in my absence.

Pech Farguet has eyes and ears, too. And what had it seen and heard in the course of its nearly two-hundred-year history? Whom had it watched come and go before these foreigners—the English couple and now this American? Who had called it home? Finding out who my predecessors were would provide a kind of genealogy: I would know where I came from. And I now felt I owed this house something: honor and respect for what it was.

Since the house is so small, I had imagined it as a former worker's cottage, or perhaps a storage barn of a larger estate or farm. There was also an intriguing passage in the Pinckney letter: "According to Madame Bru the old cottage was moved up from below about seventy-five years ago. Personally, all I think they brought up was the large cornerstones and most of the woodwork. I have never encountered any conclusive evidence on the subject." What on earth could this mean?

The questions began to dog me. Who would know?

I started with Madame Sanchez at the *mairie*. It was late morning and no one else was there requiring her attention. She rose with a smile of recognition, though it had been nearly three years since we'd met over the water business. I stated my purpose: to track the owners of my house. I half expected a sigh of hopelessness: there would be forms to fill out, a bureaucratic maze to negotiate, months—years?—awaiting approval, and so on. Instead, she nodded agreeably. From the back room, she brought out several enormous, ancient books, which looked to me as if they belonged in a museum. Yet she leafed and riffled through them as if they were no more precious than paperbacks. In elegant brown script, the properties were listed according to owners.

Madame Sanchez had the bloodhound instincts of a born researcher. In fact, she became so caught up in her quest that she seemed to forget my presence. I didn't say a word as I watched her work: mumbling names and dates to herself, scurrying back and forth from the back room, digging out more documents, and making hasty notes on a piece of paper. This went on for over an hour. I was diverted by photographs of Carennac schoolchildren hanging on one wall, from 1918, 1928, and 1931. I find old photographs of people both riveting and disturbing, as if the camera stopped life, froze them in time. They stare back at us across the years: once we were young, they say, with the world before us. Now we are old; some of us have passed away. This is the only testimony to who we were.

If I could find out who had lived in Pech Farguet, the records would stand as testimony: this is who we were.

At one point during Madame Sanchez's research, a young gentleman, apparently a salesman of computer equipment, dropped in. He didn't get far with his pitch. She was too busy, another time, she told him distractedly. An elderly gentleman followed on his heels; she greeted him enthusiastically. Perhaps he could shed some light on the mystery of who had lived at Pech Farguet? He shook his head disconsolately at the unreliability of his memory. It was too long ago. She never asked this gentleman's business, and after a patient ten-minute wait he went away.

Eventually, Madame Sanchez organized her findings on a single piece of paper and handed it to me. Her handwriting was in the same rather florid style of the Bézamats' and Hirondes', as if they'd all learned penmanship from the same nun. Here's how it read:

> 1841   M Frène Jean
> 1849   M Bayssen Jean (peutêtre 2 filles)
> 1872   M Malbet Antoine, gendre de M Bayssen Jean
> 1888   M Bouat Jean, gendre de M Bayssen Jean
> 1943   Mme Bouat Jean (veuve)
> 1966   Mme Lasfargues née Bouat
>   Mme Trémouille née Bouat
>   (2 filles de M et Mme Bouat Jean)
> 1969   M Pinckney

I pored over this amazing list. Madame Sanchez reviewed it for me. Monsieur Jean Bayssen, she explained, probably had two daughters; Antoine Malbet and Jean Bouat would have been his sons-in-law. At Jean Bouat's death, his widow inherited the house, but, she added, she hadn't lived there. The house was unoccupied for years and years during that period. (This would accord with Gabrielle Servais's recollection that during the war my house had served as a refuge, which made sense given its high vantage point and camouflage of woods.) When the two daughters inherited the property at her death, it continued to remain unoccupied, since they had married and lived elsewhere with their husbands.

Could she guess what the men's occupations would have been? I asked. *"Paysans,"* she said simply. Farmers. What would they make of me? What would they think of the transformation of Pech Farguet? I imagined them standing in a line outside the house, their faces ruddy and weathered, their rough hands soiled from labor in the fields. Jean Frène, Jean Bayssen, Antoine Malbet, Jean Bouat. *"Je suis heureuse de faire votre connaissance,"* I say, in my proper schoolgirl's French. They extend their elbows out of politeness. But I shake their hands, feeling the gritty earth. I invite them in and they are surprised, amazed at the look of the place. They nod at me, smiling in approval.

I thanked Madame Sanchez for giving me so much time. Come back, she offered, when she had more time and she would trace it further. The house was much older, of course, surely dating back to the early part of the nineteenth century.

I'd never experienced the pleasure of research before—my education had been one long process of rote memorization, it seemed—and I'd caught something of the thrill of it. It was akin, I guessed, to an archaeological dig, unearthing the mysteries of the past. Madame Sanchez's efforts had yielded a bare outline. I wanted flesh and bones. Perhaps there was more I could ferret out.

I decided to pay a call on Jean Mas, the *notaire* whose office is on a nondescript side street in Puybrun and who officiated at the closing of my house. Perhaps he could add to these skeletal details. I rang the bell and soon heard footsteps trundling down the stairs. The old wooden door was opened by a middle-aged woman who escorted me up the stairs to the waiting room.

Monsieur Mas is a tiny, pencil-thin man, but he has the presence of a giant, with a frigid air that instills in me a sense of inferiority. He dresses impeccably, with vest and silk tie. Yes, he remembered me as the *propriétaire* of Pech Farguet. He invited me to sit in the stiff leather chair in front of his desk. He remained standing before me in a posture suggesting that I get to the point. I explained hurriedly that I wanted to trace the history of my house and who had lived there. He pursed his lips and clasped his hands in a prayerlike gesture. He explained that he had drawn up that information for Mr. Pinckney, but that it had been a costly procedure. He was not in a position to divulge this same information to me.

I was stymied. Should I offer something for access to this information? Couldn't he pass it on to me—he'd already done the research, after all—for some nominal fee? Or was there some fuzzy moral issue involved here that escaped me? Confused and uncertain, I merely expressed my regret. What might he suggest? I asked him, if I wanted to pursue this.

"*Madame Trémouille, à Carennac,*" he said, in a low tone, as if in an aside to someone else in the room. Nothing more. Just Madame Trémouille, at Carennac. Then he drew himself up and anointed me with an officious smile. "*Bonne journée,*" he said to conclude our meeting.

I tripped down the stairs. Madame Trémouille. So, the woman who had inherited the house in 1966 lived in Carennac! I savored this new bit of information, feeling like Nancy Drew.

The next day I went back to Madame Sanchez. The lunch hour was fast approaching—as usual when I have important business.

I told her I would like to meet Madame Trémouille. *"Elle habite Carennac, n'est-ce pas?"*

Madame replied that she was just about to close up and that she would lead me to the house.

She locked the office and we set off at a brisk pace around the corner toward the center of the village. I was breathless. I hadn't quite expected such immediate action and was suddenly tremulous at the thought of actually meeting the woman. We walked along the street, one that I'd strolled along time and again, that led to the church. When we reached the house, she rapped on one of the doors, beautifully carved in wood with a brass hand for a knocker. No one was home. I was half relieved. Now I had time to prepare myself.

Madame Sanchez and I parted, and I drove home for lunch. The weekend slipped past and on Monday I drove into Carennac to Madame Trémouille's house. An elderly woman, perhaps in her late seventies, opened the door. She had snow-white hair, but was tall, sturdily upright, and robust. I introduced myself and she invited me in. I'd always been curious about the interiors of the village houses. (In fact, I've always been curious about the interiors of houses in general, harking back perhaps to the Christine experience.) The door opened directly into the living room, with its stuffed chairs and a general clutter of magazines and newspapers. When I explained my purpose, she smiled kindly but said she remembered very little of those days. It would be better to talk to her older sister, Madame Virginie Lasfargues. She lived in Mézel, around four kilometers away. I thanked her and bowed out. This was somewhat disappointing, and baffling. Why couldn't she tell me anything? Why would her older sister know more than she?

I located Mézel on my map and drove there directly. The village was at the end of a steep incline. I parked Charleston and approached several workmen smoking in the sun by their truck. They pointed up a narrow footpath that climbed even higher. I struggled up the rocky passage. At the summit was a small house with a stone patio. I rang the bell, which set off the usual dog alarm. After some minutes the door opened a crack. Madame Lasfargues was stooped and wizened, surely in her late eighties.

I explained, slowly, rather loudly, for her head was pitched forward and tilted as if she was hard of hearing, that I presently owned the house in which she had grown up.

She replied in a raspy, quavering voice that she could hear me quite well. What I felt would be extraordinary news to her seemed of little interest.

Over the yaps of the little white mutt, I asked her if she could tell me anything about the house.

She closed the door behind her and toddled to the stone wall that overlooked the valley. She couldn't have been more than five feet tall; in her loose gray dress and brown shawl, she was a mere sparrow. As we stood in the sunlight I could see the gray film of her cataractous eyes behind her glasses. She looked off to the distance, as if she'd forgotten my purpose. I followed her gaze to the river below.

Her grandparents, she said, had owned the house. Did she know who had built it? She had no idea. Her grandfather had been a tenant farmer, who worked on land across the *causse*. Perhaps he had been *en métayage*, I suspected, sharing the crop with the owner. After his death, the house passed to his son, her father, who was also a farmer. Her family included a younger sister and brother, she said. I remarked that it was a small house for five people. The present garage, she explained, had formerly been another room.

She had been born in the house, while her sister had been born in Gintrac. Both she and her sister had married and moved away from home. When her parents died, the house quite naturally passed on to the son, her brother, who by then had married. (Madame Sanchez's records had skipped a beat.) When he died—no, she couldn't remember the year—she and her sister decided to sell the house, since they'd established a life with their husbands elsewhere. The Pinckneys bought the house. (So, it would seem, Madame Bru's speculation about the house's being moved from the valley was ill-founded.)

She fell silent and stood dazedly, snared in the cobwebs of memory. I bent down and commented on the beautiful view of the river from her house. She took off her glasses, as if to take in an unfiltered perspective.

"*Même avec ces vieux yeux,*" she said wryly. Even with these old eyes.

In the fall, I was back at the *mairie*. It was a crisp, sunny morning. The fog in the valley, which I always regard with despair from my bedroom window, had already burned off, as it usually does, to my continual amazement. The muffled chant of the schoolchildren swelled from the classroom. The trees in the courtyard were just turning color, rustling in the strong breeze. (I can never look at such animated trees without thinking of my friend Leslie, who, as a child, thought the leaves stirred up the wind, rather than the reverse—a brilliant child's interpretation of a phenomenon of nature, it struck me, and a cornerstone of her particular brand of wisdom.)

Madame Sanchez agreed to continue digging into my house's history, but she said that she couldn't offer a great deal of hope. The records might not go much further back than we'd seen before. Out came the books, and like a groundhog she began tunneling through them again, one by one, back and forth, peering down through her green-and-blue-speckled bifocals.

After a half hour or so of this, a tall, handsome gentleman entered and joined her behind the counter. She briefly explained her mission to him. He smiled at me in a sympathetic, mild-mannered way and started perusing the books himself, as if he'd caught our fever. Eventually, between them, they traced the ownership of Jean Frène further back, to 1824. But that was as far as the books took them. Then, having identified the plot of Pech Farguet as No. 854, they resorted to maps, plowing through a stack in a cabinet by the window. At the bottom, the oldest map, from 1816, indeed had the number etched in a faint chicken scratch of ink. I ran my hand over the rough, heavy, cream-colored paper in awe. Shouldn't these be under lock and key, in a climate-controlled storeroom?

That was the best they could do, they said in accord, with a shrug of shoulders. Monsieur said that in all likelihood, the house predated 1816, but surely would have been owned by Frène or his father. I was satisfied.

I bowed to Madame Sanchez and thanked her for all the time she'd spent on my behalf. Tracking down the previous owners of the house gave me a sense of continuity; the specific names and dates were the building blocks on which I stood. I felt a link with the past, rooted. I nodded to Monsieur and said, congenially, that I hadn't realized that he worked at the office along with Madame.

Yes, he said, as if he'd swallowed a frog, I work here because I'm the mayor! He extended his hand. Evariste Marty, he said, introducing himself and managing to maintain his aplomb.

Madame's smile was a perfect red bow.

18

THE FILM

"*Je suis crevée de fatigue*," I announced to Raymond when I met him at the station. It was an emphatic way of stating my feeling of exhaustion—literally, I'm croaking from fatigue—that I'd recently learned in my French class. It was the perfect moment to test it out, jet- and train-lagged as I was.

"*Nous disons 'morte de fatigue,'* " he replied, with emphasis on the *morte*, as we headed for the car. I understood this as a sort of minor correction. Raymond's version was exactly as we'd say it in English: dead tired. But why hadn't my expression worked?

(When I later told my teacher, Huguette, who is from Paris, she was tickled. "Ah," she explained, "there's Paris French and there's country French. They're often more proper in the country.")

It was October 1994. As we drove off, Raymond took a route other than our usual one from St-Dénis to Carennac. I asked him why he was taking this direction.

"*À cause du film,*" he said, with a sideward glance.

A film? This escaped my understanding.

Oui. He nodded vigorously. A film was being made in Carennac.

My first reaction was one of horror—the film industry descending on, invading, the village! *My* village.

Raymond, however, was ebullient. He explained that the film was for a television series that would be aired in the spring. It was based on a novel, *La Rivière Espérance*, the first part of a historical trilogy by Christian Signol, who, he said, is one of France's most popular and prolific writers. The river, he related, is the Dordogne. The story is about the coming-of-age of a thirteen-year-old boy named Benjamin Donnadieu, who joins his father, the captain of several barges (*gabares*, as they were called), in his business of shipping wood from Souillac to the viticulturists in Bordeaux. Souillac would not do as a setting for the film, however, because the town had been modernized. Carennac had been chosen for its resemblance to villages of the early nineteenth century, where the story is set.

I winced again. Would the film transform Carennac somehow? I had a vision of zealous television viewers piling in the family car for a look at the site, of entrepreneurs setting up boutiques, of fast-food franchise operators, of God knows what.

Then, in a rather shy aside, Raymond mentioned that he would be appearing in the film. I shrieked in delight: "*Une vedette!*" No, he was no star, he said gravely, apologetically—he hadn't meant to mislead me. He was only in the background. He explained that months prior to the filming (they'd only been shooting for a week and expected to continue through the month of October), placards had been posted all around and advertisements had appeared in the papers for locals who might want to apply for bit parts. Three hundred had applied and sixty-one had been chosen; only a half dozen were women, who had to have long hair to qualify. Priority had been given to residents of Carennac. He had had to fill out a form stating his name, age, identity number, profession, and clothing size; this had to be accompanied by a photograph. He'd been chosen to portray an old man of the village who watches the goings-on at the port; his costume consisted of pantaloons, a *chemise* with pleats and lace cuffs, a vest and jacket, and a linen cap. He'd been asked to grow a beard. He didn't know what the pay would be, but he'd heard that one of his neighbors, who was required to drive a tractor, had been handsomely compensated.

It would be like Raymond Hironde, I thought—the most gregarious and adventurous of my neighbors—to be the first to sign up. My worry about the ruin the film might cause evaporated. This was going to be great fun! I'd planned to take an excursion to the Auvergne for a few days at a mountain spa, but I immediately scratched the trip. The spa would be there next year. I wasn't going to miss this.

We approached the village from the far end. Raymond pointed ahead to the string of trucks lining the road, which, he explained, were all connected to the film: one for makeup, one for costumes, and so on. A big canteen was stationed by the abbey. They were in the process of filming at the moment. Did I want to stop and have a look?

Raymond parked the car and we walked up the road to the village. It had started to rain, a fine mist. There was a small cluster of people on the bridge, the women huddled under umbrellas. I gasped at the sight far below on the shore of the river. Several *gabares*, with their sails lashed, were anchored at a newly constructed pier. A number of figures in period costume—a woman, several young children, a man—moved idly around the pier. Two donkeys stood with bent heads, munching nonchalantly. Raymond said that the boats, the pier, and a wooden warehouse *(entrepôt)* that I couldn't see from this angle had all been especially built for the film. A stern voice suddenly trumpeted *"en place"* through a megaphone and the crowd on the bridge, tittering, echoed the command. *"Silence!"* a young woman standing at the end of the bridge and armed with headphones, hissed officiously.

The mist and the gray, waning light created a romantic atmosphere. The stand of trees on the island formed an Impressionist-like backdrop. The village had been returned to what it once was. I stood transfixed while Raymond chatted with his friends.

On the drive to the house, Raymond explained that he was constantly on call. They filmed every day; it was possible that he'd be called tomorrow, a Saturday. The hours were long. He might be summoned for two o'clock in the afternoon and have to be on hand past midnight.

After marketing in Brive on Saturday morning, I drove immediately to St-Céré to pick up a copy of the Signol book. Not surprisingly, it was prominently displayed at the bookstore, along with the other two books in the trilogy, *Le Royaume du Fleuve* and *L'Âme de la Vallée*. It was a large paperback, with an aerial-view color photograph of the Dordogne. A short biography of the author stated that he was in a long line of great popular romantic writers in France and lived in Brive. I greedily considered buying all three books, but restrained myself. *La*

Rivière would be enough to keep me occupied through the week.

On the way home, I stopped at the Hirondes. It was only eleven in the morning, but Simone was busy preparing lunch for Raymond. He'd received a call the night before asking him to show up at noon, she said excitedly, and he hadn't even gotten into costume. Raymond sat at the table, his hands clasped before him. He appeared totally unruffled and deflected, with a gruff cough, my enthusiasm. I asked Simone if she would be going to watch the proceedings, and she suggested we meet a bit later—"*sur le pont*"—at around two o'clock. I went home for lunch and plunged into the book.

I brought an umbrella—it was sprinkling again—binoculars, and a notebook. Simone was already on the bridge when I arrived precisely at two o'clock. On the "set" at the pier below, she pointed out the director—an overweight, imposing figure in a baseball cap, holding a megaphone, and the author himself, a tall, handsome, middle-aged gentleman with his hands jammed in his pants pockets and his shoulders hunched inside his windbreaker. I gazed through the binoculars and then passed them to Simone, who was impressed by their incredible range. She passed them on to several other ladies gathered on the bridge.

Simone explained that her brother and sister-in-law, Michel and Thérèse Fraysse, lived to the left of the bridge in a house that overlooked the river and the reconstructed port. It was one of the most charming old houses in the village and I'd often admired it. The filmmakers had instructed them to keep the curtains closed at all times, though they managed to peek through a crack to get a bird's-eye view of the action. Simone suggested that I go

down and have a look at the set by taking the path leading down to the river. They would leave the door of the
house unlocked so that I could drop in at any point.

I trundled down the path, while Simone went to the
house. To the left I could now see the reconstructed warehouse, with a sign that read *ENTREPÔT LOMBARD* (the
name of a well-to-do merchant I recognized as a character from the book). I stood on its huge wooden porch and
glanced back overhead to the Fraysses' house. Simone
was peeking through the curtains and gave a little surrep-
titious wave.

On the river, a small rubber raft plied back and forth
with a portable machine emitting an atmospheric fog. An
early passage in the book recounts Benjamin's impression
of the Dordogne, and this description was now unrolling
before my very eyes. It translates:

> He went out into the weak dawn which was filled
> with the smell of water. It was a familiar smell, but this
> morning, it seemed heavier and made you feel as if you
> could suffocate. It might seem like an exhalation of
> mud, pebbles, sand, gravel, moss, roots, leaves, fish, a
> sweetish but powerful flux which touched your lips
> and made one feel like tasting it. The true smell of the
> Dordogne, the smell of its lithe as well as muscular
> body, of its supple legs, its caressing arms, its hair of
> green algae.

The great white Labrador from the Vieux Quercy inn
gamboled about, to the consternation of the film crew.
Two mules were grazing downriver. At this closer range,
I could see that the *gabares* were loaded with what were
called *piquets*, the tapered wooden posts used in the vine-

yards. The actors and actresses in costumes milled about aimlessly—except for Raymond, who was standing motionless and in grave concentration on the dock, looking very much the rugged country farmer. To the right of the *entrepôt*, the *réalisiteur* sat in the typical director's chair—clenching his fists, biting his nails, puffing on a cigar. He had long curly brown hair and wore jeans and a sweater around his shoulders. His baseball cap said SPORTY BOY, ADVENTURES IN THE WILDERNESS. He wore the requisite black sunglasses, although it was now raining fairly steadily.

"*Silence!*" he barked over the megaphone. "*En place rapidement, s'il vous plaît.*" A soundman waited nearby, holding aloft what looked like a giant dust mop. A cameraman stood at the ready with his equipment slung over his shoulder. I was struck by the fact that the film was being made with a handheld camera.

A tight band of actors, led by a large man in a black fedora and cape (Jean-Claude Drouat, in the role of Benjamin's father), strode down purposefully to the pier, trailed by the soundman and cameraman.

"*Coupez!*" the director shouted. The scenario had lasted all of a half minute. This was repeated and then the actors dispersed, except for Raymond, who remained planted at his post on the pier.

I circled back to the house. The door was open. I danced on tiptoes through the small front room, glancing furtively about. It was ill-lit, sparsely furnished, and claustrophobic because of its low ceilings—not as inviting as the house's exterior. Simone and two ladies were gathered on the enclosed back porch. She introduced me to her sisters-in-law: Thérèse, her brother's wife, and Madeleine, who was Raymond's sister. Thérèse was a tall woman with feathery, cropped white hair, piercing blue eyes, and a hawklike expression. She reminded me slightly of Phyllis Diller. She seemed ecstatic to meet me and led me by the arm, in a conspiratorial fashion, to the curtained window, where, she said, in a barely contained whisper, I could secretly observe *le tournage*. And I was invited to return, whenever I wanted, any day, anytime. Did I know, by the way, she asked, as if she was imparting only to me a well-kept secret, that Elisabeth Depardieu—*très vivante, très charmante*—was staying in the Vieux Quercy? Everyone said that her husband called her every single night. Her eyes grew wide. She chuckled wickedly and poked me gently with an elbow.

Madeleine was the spitting image of Raymond: dark-skinned, with straight brown hair, chocolate-brown eyes, and a pronounced nose. While Raymond had an avuncular look, she had the plain, unassuming appearance and shy gentleness of a spinster aunt (though I later learned she was married to the mayor of Carennac whom I'd met). Madeleine was rereading the Signol books—she seemed to have the same intellectual curiosity as her brother—and put in context for me the scene we had just witnessed. She had the most melodious voice I'd ever heard, as lyrical as her name.

It had begun to pour. The filming seemed to be at an impasse. I bowed out and made my way home.

The next day I stopped at the Hirondes. Raymond had had to stay past midnight the night before. The actors, he said with a chortle, had all let off a little steam by parading through the streets of Carennac with torches, shouting "Emmeline, Emmeline!" By now, I had read enough of the book to recognize the cast of characters. The daughter of the rich merchant Lombard, Emmeline attempts to win Benjamin from Marie, his true love since childhood. At the same time Raymond mentioned in passing the name of the director: Josée Dayan. "Josée!" I exclaimed in astonishment. He was a she. Raymond admitted that it was confusing: her masculine appearance and gruff manner—and the cigar. She ate four times the amount of any man, he added. This only increased my fascination with the whole movie business.

Each day thereafter, before I went into town, I would check at the Hirondes to see if Raymond had been called. (Several days passed without requiring his presence.) At the same time I made the rounds of the neighbors. Monsieur Bézamat simply couldn't take time out to watch the filmmaking. Madame smiled indulgently. My obsession with the film seemed to amuse them. The Servais hadn't been in to Carennac either. There was simply too much to do around the house. Serge was in the middle of restoring the fireplace, and he knew what filmmaking was like: a complete bore, the same thing over and over again. Gabrielle did say that she'd read and enjoyed all of the Signol books, but the idea of seeing them come to life on film—practically on her doorstep—didn't move her.

And so, Thérèse and I became fellow *cinéphiles*. I could find her every day, either sitting on the bench on the patio outside her house, if there was a break in filming, or observing *sur le pont* or through the curtains inside the house.

One day we were waiting for the action to begin, on one of the side streets of the village. The usual small band of curious onlookers was present. The setup was for a scene in which Benjamin makes the rounds of neighbors begging for money to free Marie's father, who was imprisoned for night fishing. We were standing just behind the director's chair: Josée was sipping coffee and munching on a croissant. I asked Thérèse what captivated her about the filmmaking.

"*J'aime l'animation!*" she said spiritedly, referring to all the activity but also, I felt, to something more intangible. Then she added, as if in the strictest confidence, that she loved to dance. Oh, how she had danced in Paris! The waltz, the cha-cha-cha, the tango, all sorts of dances. She rolled her eyes and rocked herself in her arms, as if to the sound of a distant orchestra.

I was jotting down her words in my notebook as she spoke, which pleased her enormously. She drew closer, conspiratorially. She whispered in my ear that she had had a premonition as a child that this moment would come, this great moment when she would participate in a film. (Thérèse had been assigned an upcoming small role as an old woman of the village, costumed in a black robe and headdress that made her look, she said huffily, like a mother superior.) All her life had been building to this. As a child, she'd had an intense feeling for movement and performance; her mother had recognized this. Then Thérèse stepped back and said wistfully that she might have had a career in dancing, but she'd married, moved here with Michel. She was too old to dance now. She shuddered. She dreaded the solitude of winter. Then she rallied. This moment, she nodded sagely, had been destined. "*L'animation, ah!*" That was her passion. "*J'aime l'animation!*" She folded her arms over her bosom and looked at me piercingly.

Along with a small group of people behind the director's chair, we watched the scene repeated over and over and over again. After a "*silence!*" and "*moteur*" bellowed by Josée, Benjamin (played by Aurélien Wiik) would run to the end of the road past the village houses while a peasant, on cue, led his donkey up the street. At one of the houses, where two women were leaning out of the window, Benjamin would shout his line, *"Avez-vous un peu d'argent pour payer l'amende?"* (Do you have a little money to pay the fine?) With each repetition, it sounded less and less heartfelt. The scene took perhaps three minutes. Far from bored by the repetition, Thérèse and I were hypnotized.

The author Signol hovered about, silently overseeing the proceedings. Several of the spectators approached him with a copy of the book for him to sign. Thérèse had brought a copy for signing as well—for a friend.

Before we knew it, the afternoon had slipped away. I was curious, though, whether everyone was as happy with the filmmaking as Thérèse. Surely all this *animation* would seem disruptive to some of the villagers: the trucks and paraphernalia, the strictures, the late-night filming. I decided to get two other points of view, one negative and one positive.

For the former, Simone advised me, I should talk to Monsieur Rougier, who lived on the road above town, just past the *mairie*.

I met Monsieur Rougier just as he was pedaling home on his bicycle. When I explained my purpose, he immediately invited me in. A retired schoolteacher, he was a trim, handsome man who looked younger than his years, with curly hair and glasses. As I followed him to the house I noticed that he had a pronounced limp from a deformity of his left leg, though he had the vigorous appearance of a *sportif* type. His house was a tastefully restored barn, with a modern open kitchen leading up to a spacious living room with rose-tiled floors, wooden casement windows, and a handsome wooden staircase. We sat on low cream-colored couches across from each other.

Monsieur Rougier spoke with an air of calm intelligence. He was not *against* the film, he was quick to say, but the manner of making the film. The Gaumont company had had a meeting with the villagers—it was outdoors in the center of town, with drinks served—but it was just blather. The problem was that no one was informed properly about the day-to-day proceedings, that is, when and where the filming would take place. His complaint was that the *régisseur* (the assistant director) Monsieur Christian Lambert, who was responsible for overseeing everything, had little regard for the inhabitants of the village.

Monsieur Rougier leaned back and grasped his crossed knees. It wasn't one particular thing—he shrugged—but an accumulation of many things that made him angry (though his mild manner and pleasant disposition belied this).

For example, he said, there is a ninety-three-year-old woman, a neighbor of his who lives near a *grange* he owns in the village. One morning, she told him, she opened her window for some air and was startled to see a man descending a ladder with parts of the drainage system of her house (the trappings of modernity that wouldn't be appropriate for the era of the film). When Monsieur Rougier asked Lambert why he hadn't telephoned the owner of the house, the *régisseur* responded that there hadn't been enough time.

It was nothing grave, Monsieur Rougier reiterated. Just small things. In his retirement, he said, he enjoyed fishing. But the building of the *gabares* on the river put an end to fishing in his customary spot. It was as if the filmmakers came in like conquerors and took over the village.

For the opposite point of view—one who was *ravi*—Raymond and Simone urged me to visit Monsieur Malmartel, Raymond's friend since childhood, who was a retired English professor.

Monsieur Malmartel lived in a two-story house on the main road leading into Carennac. When I rang his bell, he was in the midst of supervising a young workman who was repainting his kitchen. He escorted me into the dining room, where we sat at the table. Monsieur Malmartel was a rotund, jolly man, with a pumpkin face, ruddy cheeks, silver-framed glasses, and a little wool saucer of a cap. He explained that he had taught English for thirty years to high-school students in Brive, where he still had an apartment. He apologized that his English wasn't up to snuff; since he'd retired he'd lost the facility. I assured him that it was first-rate and told him I was surprised, in fact, that he had an American instead of a British accent. He said he'd picked it up by watching the CBS news each morning. "So, I heard, for example, that you say 'Penagon,' " which he pronounced without the *t* in a broad, nasal inflection, "rather than Pentagon,' " which he enunciated with a crisp, high-toned British inflection.

Monsieur Malmartel had read the Signol book in ten consecutive days. He found it very moving. *"On verse des larmes à toutes les pages"* (one cries over every page). I asked him if he regarded the book as popular or fine literature. (I had concluded from reading the book that it was a popular romance, epic in scope, with rather stereotypical characters and predictable action—albeit with a certain historical breadth.) Signol, he said definitively, was one of the ten best writers in France today, another Balzac. It had taken him three years to complete the book, which Monsieur found an astonishing feat.

I asked Monsieur Malmartel if he had applied for a role in the film, as had his friend Raymond Hironde.

He laughed uproariously. "No, indeed," he said. "But it's like Raymond Hironde to give himself an air of self-importance." Monsieur Malmartel drew himself up in a snobbish posture. "His father was the same way," he added, with a wicked, teasing gleam in his eyes. In fact, he had no interest in even watching the film being made. There was no time. Besides, he'd seen films made from books, and they never lived up to the original. But he did have great hopes that the film would revitalize Carennac. This launched him on an account of the state of affairs in the village.

"If we don't have at least a basic business environment, the village is lost for the future," Monsieur Malmartel pronounced solemnly. "There's not a butcher, not a baker, not a *garagiste*. Except for the hotels, we lack the commercial trades to make a living village. We don't even have facilities to make the most normal purchase. That lamp"—he pointed to a lightbulb in the chandelier—"cost ten francs here in the village. I can buy four of them for five francs in Brive. Here, so you will know I don't lie!" He sprang from his chair and pulled out a pack of four lightbulbs from a cabinet at the side of the room. He pointed to the price sticker: 4.85 francs. He sat down and rested his case, his arms crossed over his paunch.

"The single grocer is the only merchant," Monsieur Malmartel continued. "The butcher passes once a week from Miers, the baker from Bétaille two times a week. Fifty years ago there were fifteen hundred inhabitants in Carennac. Today there are three hundred, perhaps three-fifty. If you have no car, you're totally lost. A bus leaves for Brive at eight A.M. and returns at five P.M., so you must spend the whole day in Brive." He guffawed at the absurdity of this.

He wanted the film to succeed because he was a businessman. He could remember hearing the sound of the blacksmith on his way to school when he was just a boy. It was the sound of industry that you no longer heard. Monsieur Malmartel paused, as if his ear was turned to the far-off sound. The recollection of the sound tripped a memory. This reminded him, he said, of an English expression he was fond of: "The church is an anvil that has worn out many hammers." He spread his outstretched palms on the table, as if this concluded his sermonizing for one day.

When I left Monsieur Malmartel's, I considered his viewpoint, but selfishly concluded that I wanted Carennac to stay just as it was. I walked through the village, where tourists strolled about—past the canteen by the abbey, past the trucks nearly blocking the tiny streets, across the bridge, to Thérèse's house. She was excited to see me. The day before (when I'd skipped the filmmaking to visit a friend in the Périgord) she'd taken part in the film. She ran into the house to fetch a photograph and we sat on the bench on the patio. I stared at the picture, hardly recognizing Thérèse. She was outfitted in her black robe, which had a white lace ruff, and a headdress with a white band. She did, indeed, look like a mother superior. Now, I exclaimed, she would see herself on television. She looked troubled. She had been made to look so old—who would recognize her? Michel, she now informed me, had been told that he might be called to Paris, for filming in a studio there. She sighed and gazed at the bridge lined with people. *"Tout le monde,"* she said in an aside to herself—as if she'd be left with this less than stellar crowd.

My trip was drawing to an end. For the last day of

filming—Raymond had gotten the call to appear at three o'clock—I picked up Simone, who had a bag of lettuce and squash for Thérèse. On the way into town I mentioned how fond I was of Thérèse—her enthusiasm, her spirit, her talkativeness. Simone laughed and rolled her eyes. Thérèse, she moaned, can give you a headache with her talk. Her brother Michel was so calm and gentle; Thérèse was so *nerveuse.* They were happy. How to explain the mystery of human relationships? I asked Simone about Thérèse's dancing career in Paris. Oh, Simone said, she danced in the Bal de Napoléon, a dance hall where retired people came for amusement. Thérèse had danced with the retired gentlemen who frequented the place.

Thérèse had informed us that filming would not begin until five. *"C'est dingue!"* she said. I'd never heard the expression and asked her what it meant. It was a Parisian expression, she explained, similar to *"C'est fou!"* (It's crazy.) Very Parisian. (Later, I found the word in the French dictionary.) She offered Simone and me coffee and cookies, which we could take on the patio since the afternoon was so warm and sunny.

Afterward I strolled down the path to the river and walked out on the pier. Raymond and Michel were paddling down the river in a small boat to pass the time. The white Labrador frolicked about, making mad dashes into the water. Trees surrounding the *entrepôt* were decorated with ribbons and roses. On the porch, the actor who earlier had had the role of a sailor was rehearsing a group of young people in country dances to recorded fiddle music. He hammered out the steps with his voice: *"da, da-da, da . . . da, da-da, da . . . daa, daa, daa."* The couples—presumably untrained local youngsters—laughed with embarrassment as they clumsily followed his lead. A trio of musicians in costume were huddled on a bench reviewing handwritten sheet music. The scene was to be a celebration of the feast of St. Jean, which occurs at the summer solstice. I recalled the delightful passage in the book in which Marie, despondent at Benjamin's absence, overcomes a reluctance to dance and joins the revelers, singing a refrain she had often heard since childhood:

> *Quand dans le ciel brille l'étoile*
> *Que le jour nous dit adieu*
> *Que la lune toute rousse*
> *Se prélasse dans les cieux . . .*

> *(When the star shines in the sky*
> *When the day tells us good-bye*
> *When the moon all russet*
> *basks in the heavens . . .)*

When I returned to Thérèse's house, Raymond and Michel had received word that the scene wouldn't be filmed until later in the evening. Simone and I said farewell. On the way home in the car, Simone muttered, *"C'est dingue!"* smiling softly. *"C'est dingue!"*

That evening was clear and still, the darkened heavens flooded with stars. On the pier, the boats and trees, illuminated with lamps, were festooned with ribbons and flowers that barely fluttered on the gentle air. The dancers wore fancy, colorful dress. The fiddlers bowed their repetitive music; its old-fashioned melodies saddened me. The dancers stomped and twirled, now polished, graceful, and gay. The people gathered on the bridge were mostly silent, moved beyond speech, or spoke in a soft murmur. The gaiety brought a lump to your throat. You wished

you were young. You wished that you had been born yes-
teryear, when Carennac was this enchanting every day
and the world was less complicated. Your heart yearned
for life so sweet. Monsieur Malmartel appeared. We continued to watch, as the music and dancing cast its spell.
At a pause, Monsieur Malmartel said quietly that this
was the most beautiful moment Carennac had ever seen.

And then we made our way home through the magical
night.

ABOUT THE AUTHOR

A former editor at *The New Yorker* and *The New York Times*, ANN BARRY wrote extensively on travel and food. She died in 1996.

Printed in the United States
30892LVS00001B/115-117